THE QUEEN ANNE HOUSE

America's Victorian Vernacular

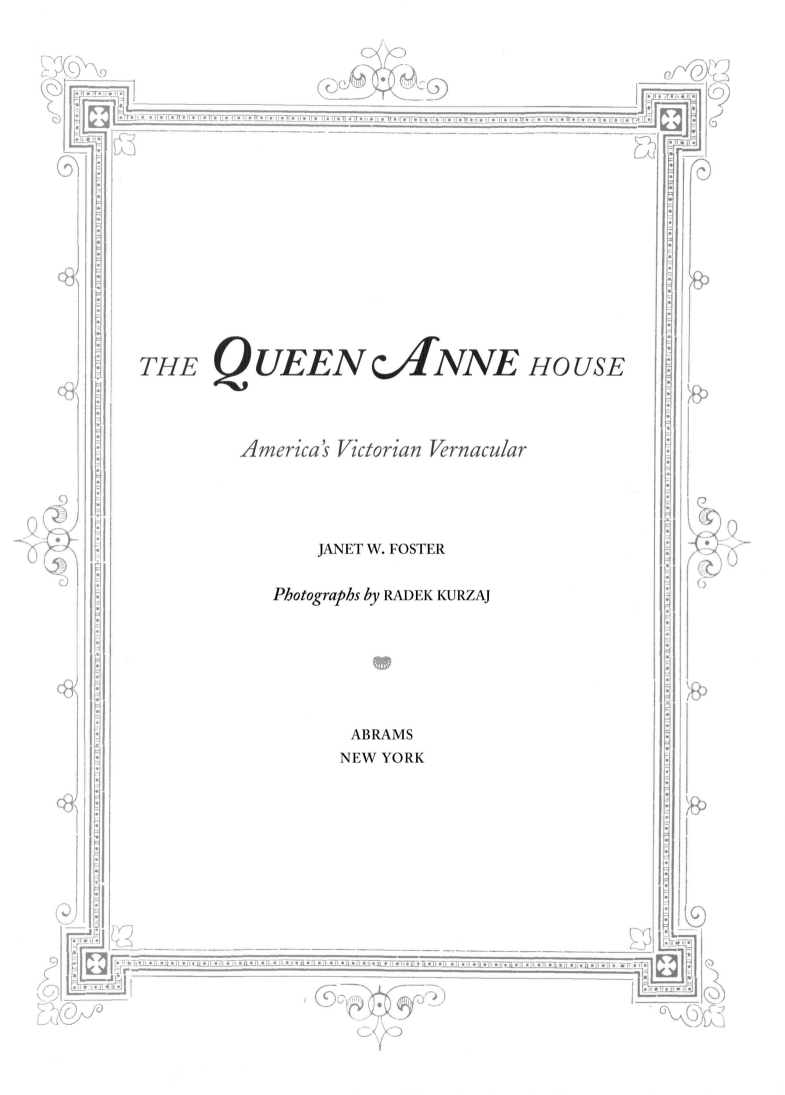

THE QUEEN ANNE HOUSE

America's Victorian Vernacular

JANET W. FOSTER

Photographs by RADEK KURZAJ

ABRAMS

NEW YORK

PROJECT MANAGER: Harriet Whelchel

EDITOR: KB Mello

DESIGNER: Emily Waters

PRODUCTION MANAGER: Jane Searle

Library of Congress Cataloging-in-Publication Data

Foster, Janet W.
  The Queen Anne house : America's Victorian vernacular / Janet W. Foster ; photography by Radek Kurzaj.
    p. cm.
  Includes bibliographical references and index.
  ISBN 0-8109-3085-4 (hardcover)
  1. Architecture, Domestic--United States--19th century. 2. Queen Annerevival (Architecture)--United
States. 3. Vernacular architecture--United States--19th
century. I. Title.

  NA7207.F67 2006
  728.80973
                    2006010842

Published in 2006 by Abrams,
an imprint of Harry N. Abrams, Inc.

Printed and bound in China
10 9 8 7 6 5 4 3 2 1

HNA ▉▉▉▉
harry n. abrams, inc.
a subsidiary of La Martinière Groupe
115 West 18th Street
New York, NY 10011
www.hnabooks.com

PREVIOUS PAGE: *Watts Sherman House, Newport, Rhode Island.*

PAGE 6: *Entry, Edward Brooke House, Birdsboro, Pennsylvania.*

PAGE 7: *View from second floor of Piatt House, Tunkhannock, Pennsylvania.*

CONTENTS

INTRODUCTION

IN 1884, *The Brooklyn Daily Eagle*, the daily newspaper of what was, at the time, the third largest city in the United States, published an article titled "The Multiplication of Queen Anne Houses."[1] The article described the phenomenal growth and development of Brooklyn, and the creation of extraordinary new buildings in a new style of architecture.

The article begins: "A number of what are called Queen Anne or Elizabethan houses going up in the most fashionable quarters of Brooklyn is on the increase, and their dormers and peaked gables and light serial balconies make bright and pretty pictures here and there along the thoroughfares. …These showy and semi-fantastic constructions, rich with stained glass and carvings and rococo traceries culminating in a wilderness of pinnacles…are likewise built on the high ground between Brooklyn and New York." Thus the article put together for the average reader a description of the most notable features of a new architectural expression and its most common name.

In the mid-1880s, Queen Anne style was reaching its height of popularity and the climax of its development as a distinctive architectural form, a development that had begun in the United States only a decade earlier. The first Queen Anne–style house in the United States is generally agreed upon by architectural historians as the Watts Sherman House in Newport, Rhode Island, designed by Henry Hobson Richardson in 1874–1875.

Yet within a few years of the laudatory prose noted above, *The Brooklyn Daily Eagle* was more critical of houses in the style, as in this article from December 27, 1891:

> It is perhaps safe to say that no previous year has been marked by such
> extreme departures from orthodox standards in architectural designs…
> The city has been rendered vastly more spectacular by those radical departures
> from the familiar types of building, whether or not it has everywhere been
> made more beautiful… [The observer] may rest assured that though all of
> its different features will be of familiar types he will never have seen them
> combined as in this house.

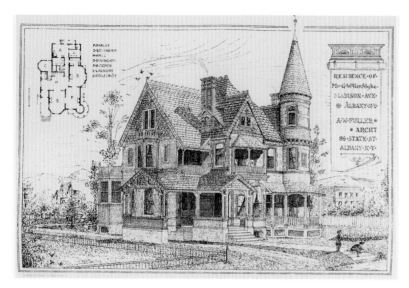

The classic American Queen Anne–style house, with its gables, turrets, porches, and variety of materials, was fully formed and widely published by 1880, when this image appeared in the magazine The American Architect and Building News.

By the dawn of the twentieth century, Queen Anne had run its course, and it entered an era of unpopularity and disparagement from the public press. *The Brooklyn Daily Eagle* stated: "... grotesque and sometimes hideous construction of a higglety-pigglety class of architecture in which every style was mixed up and no type either predominated or appeared to good effect. ...architects who were responsible for this fantastic effect called their creations Queen Anne, for want of a better name. ...in truth, there is no actual Queen Anne style."[2]

But of course there was—it was just unfashionable by the time this critique was written, against the backdrop of the rising popularity of classicism and the Colonial Revival style. The Queen Anne style's very insistence on ornament, on plasticity of form, on integral color, and on a multiplicity of design sources for details made it an easy target for those who preferred classicism, symmetry, and rationality in architecture.

The Queen Anne–style house marks both the high point and the end of the Victorian era of elaborately decorative architecture, and also the real beginning of domestic comfort and the "modern" house. It embodies a catch-all of architectural features from around the world, and yet it evolved to become a distinctive and recognizable part of American architecture. The Queen Anne style is not included in some academic architectural histories of the United States, obscured by its high-style cousins the Shingle Style and the Romanesque Revival style, but it certainly existed for a quarter century as one of the most popular national styles of architecture, particularly for domestic buildings.

Contradictory, undisciplined, exuberant, and expressive, the Queen Anne style may just be the best example of a national vernacular architectural style produced in the United States. It arose from high-minded architectural sources, but it evolved into a commercially-popularized form transmitted by builders and magazine articles more often than through serious architectural journals. Vernacular architecture, that is, the buildings produced outside the realm of groundbreaking, high-style architectural design, and created with the talents and materials most readily available in a locale, has always comprised the bulk of the built environment.

American settlers brought with them the building traditions of their home countries, so that the earliest architecture in the colonies reflected quite accurately the vernacular building traditions of the region of Europe where the settlers, or more accurately, the builders among them, had come from. Time-honored building traditions were tempered with new materials, a new climate, and the manpower limits of a small population intent on developing a sprawling wilderness as quickly as possible. Thus American regional vernacular architecture was created, with differences as distinctive as the accents of the people who lived there. The saltbox house form of New England, with its massive center chimney, was quite different from the southern houses with chimneys placed outside the mass of the house. In the eighteenth century, brick patterned-end houses built by Quakers in South Jersey defined the history and geography of a community, just as banked barns and fieldstone houses did for the German communities of religious nonconformists who settled during that time in Pennsylvania.

With the creation of a new body politic after the American Revolution also came the creation of arts and industry that strived to be independent and uniquely American. Beginning with the establishment of a federal government at the creation of the Constitution in 1787, citizens worked hard to define themselves in terms of this large vision that was "The United States of America." Though the influence of European ideas was strong on the Revolutionary generation—and how could it not be, as they had all been born as Europeans, either in the Old World or its colonies—the push to create something uniquely their own was on. In architecture, it tended toward simplification of European models, both as a practical result of having fewer craftsmen trained through a guild system to a high degree of proficiency, and the economics of a country where there were no princes to sponsor elaborate palaces.

The old vernacular forms were not entirely abandoned—after all, there was still the fact that North Carolina was, on balance, warmer than Massachusetts—but there was certainly a conscious adoption of new styles, if only at the most superficial level, in order to make traditional building "modern" and "American." Wood, abundant and easily worked, became the most common material for American houses. Used as framing, sheathing, roofing, and for decorative embellishments, wood formed the basis for American vernacular architecture through the nineteenth century, and was instrumental in giving the Queen Anne style its uniquely American interpretation.

Through the nineteenth century, the number and variety of architectural styles that washed up on American shores from European antecedents increased, and all were adapted to a wooden architectural form and detailing, unlike the masonry precedents on which it was based. The Greek Revival, the Italianate, and the Gothic Revival were among the most popular styles of architecture to develop vigorous vernacular expressions before the Civil War. Today, there is a tendency to consider all the rich variety of Revival styles, emerging from the Romantic movement in all the arts, as "Victorian;" their wooden trim is the "gingerbread" of common speech. "Victorian" conjures an image of intricate decoration, richly layered color, and pattern and texture, and perhaps a quality of fussiness. But "Victorian" is not a style; rather it is a time period, referring to the reign of that great Queen upon England's throne (1837–1901). Chronologically, the Queen Anne style spans the last third of the reign of Queen Victoria and of course

"Grim's Dyke," country house in Sussex, England, was designed by Richard Norman Shaw in 1872. Shaw's country houses were intended to evoke medieval English design, but they became the basis for the American Queen Anne–style house, which incorporated many modern technologies into historicizing exteriors.

neither sovereign ever set foot in the United States or designed a house here. But certainly today in popular usage, a house described as "Victorian" might well be Queen Anne, where all the decorative and technological impulses of the period came together with a broad inclusiveness for the world's architectural forms. No wonder there is confusion in the architecture world!

The so-called Queen Anne style in architecture did have its start in England, but not until the 1860s, rather than the 1710s, when Queen Anne herself held the throne. Its development was led by the English architects Richard Norman Shaw, W. Eden Nesfield, and Phillip Webb. They saw, and bemoaned, the demise of traditional craftsmanship, and the destruction of medieval cottages and halls in the ongoing industrialization of Britain during the nineteenth century. They sought to revive the old ways, the true "English" style of building, as they saw it expressed in the architecture of the early eighteenth century. Shaw and his contemporaries looked back to a time when England was more culturally homogenous and indigenous, and before "foreign" classicism had so completely influenced the country's architecture, to the years when Queen Anne (reigned 1702–1714) was on the throne. She was not synonymous with architecture in her day, as were her successors, the Georges I through IV, who gave us the Georgian style. When she is remembered at all for her contribution to eighteenth-century design, it is for the simplified Baroque forms in furnishings that came into vogue during her reign. For Richard Norman Shaw and other architectural innovators of mid-nineteenth-century England, Queen Anne's reign was most important as the last time England was agricultural, rural, prosperous, and peaceful. In other words, the Victorians perceived the era of Queen Anne as the Romantic opposite of their own industrialized, urbanizing, and modernizing world.

Medieval, particularly Gothic, architecture had been used for much of the nineteenth century to invoke a preindustrial, spiritually rich, and hand-crafted world, but it was limited in creating usable modern residences. Looking back to the vernacular buildings of the seventeenth and eighteenth centuries provided more useful models, and as they themselves were expressions of architectural eclecticism, they provided an expansive vocabulary with which to inspire the Victorian-era Queen Anne architects. Half-timbering, casement windows, irregular rooflines, and asymmetrical elevations were features on authentic Queen Anne–era (and earlier) period houses in England. By the mid-nineteenth century these were old houses, with additions giving them even more irregular plans and rooflines. Some houses had patches and repairs that didn't match original areas, thus creating an impression of multiple materials and textures. Medievalizing features, like a second floor projecting out over the first floor and intricately patterned chimneys, were joined with rudimentary classical features, such as columns flanking a front door.

CERTAINLY AMERICANS traveled to England in the 1860s and 70s, but those who went to the remote countryside of England to see and sketch houses, and then went on to become influential architects made up a small circle indeed. Crucial to the linking of English and American Queen Anne architecture was Henry Hobson Richardson (1838–1886), one of the first Americans to train at one of the nineteenth century's most prestigious schools of architecture, L'Ecole des Beaux Arts in Paris. He followed his formal studies with a visit to England, sketching buildings he saw and admired. Richardson's genius and influence places him squarely as the paterfamilias of American architecture. He was employer and mentor to Stanford White; the first to construct a house based on the Shavian manor houses (the Watts Sherman House), which gave rise to both Shingle Style and the Queen Anne vernacular; and originator of the Romanesque Revival style in America which became affectionately known as Richardsonian Romanesque for his profound influence on its development. As a founder of the American Institute of Architects, Richardson personally transmitted ideas about the English Queen Anne to New York and Boston architectural circles in the 1870s.

English architect Richard Norman Shaw was a successful and productive architect, whose own style changed during his lifetime. His work of the 1870s was more commercial and urban in location, demanding a change from the rambling half-timber forms that were so adaptable to country houses. Shaw became associated with the term "Queen Anne" only when he turned to the simplified Baroque classicism of the early eighteenth century and used decorative elements—such as pediments, scrolls, and urns—on buildings of brick with limestone and terracotta trim. Shaw's commercial building, The New Zealand Chambers, a London trading-house of 1872, was widely praised for its use of brick, stone, and tile, and would have been seen in its published form by American builders and architects. But the commercial, urban examples of English Queen Anne Revival architecture had a limited application and following in the United States. Chiefly practiced by trained English architects who emigrated to the urban East Coast, there are examples in apartment houses in Manhattan and Brooklyn, and in expensive townhouses in the Back Bay section of Boston. But these buildings were erected for the most part for sophisticated clients with generous budgets. The materials and forms did not translate easily to the American vernacular landscape. Instead, the masonry interpretation of "Queen Anne" in England was refreshed and recast under Henry Hobson Richardson in the United States in his development of what came to be known as the Richardsonian Romanesque. This solid, masonry interpretation of Romanesque architecture, avoided, like the English Queen Anne, the influence of both the Gothic and the classical styles in its development of a new style for the new age. Perhaps just as idiosyncratic as Shaw's Queen Anne, Richardsonian Romanesque was nevertheless more simple and geometric in form and massing, and therefore more comprehensible to American builders and their clients. It is not that it was undecorated—on the contrary, it could include the most decorative elements yet seen in American architecture—but the decoration was integral to the building itself. ❀

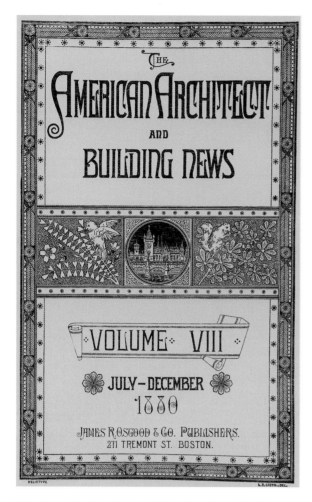

The decorative frontispiece of The American Architect and Building News, *an architectural magazine founded in Boston in 1876, about the same time the Queen Anne style was developing in the United States. Although the editors of the magazine initially promoted the style, they soon spent more ink decrying it, even as it gained popularity in the non-architectural press and with the public.*

This vocabulary was used quite differently by English architects. Phillip Webb absorbed the lessons of the preindustrial house to build "The Red House," celebrated as a forerunner of the Arts and Crafts movement. Early in his career, in the 1860s, Richard Norman Shaw designed country houses incorporating many of the details that he saw on old houses in rural England. Shaw's new country houses were big, expansive places that spread across the land in all directions. The results, houses like "Leyswood" (1868), and "Grim's Dyke" (1869), used traditional English cottage decorative elements on large, modern houses, and it was this strain of the English Queen Anne movement that most directly influenced American architects and builders. Although he never called these houses Queen Anne, the name was soon applied by others, and Shaw became known as a "Queen Anne" architect in England and in the United States.

The American Queen Anne style can be traced then to Shaw in England, and to American Henry Hobson Richardson's interpretation of British design in the United States, but its full development as a unique expression of American domestic architecture rests in the hands of the American builders, steeped in wooden construction and the American vernacular tradition.

Mostly, American architects and designers learned of the developments in English architecture through engravings and drawings, as they were published in the architectural press. Most notable during the years when Shaw was creating his interpretation of the Queen Anne style, were the English magazines, *The Builder* and *Building News*. In 1876, however, the "Queen Anne" came to America, in the form of the British government's exhibition of three buildings at the Centennial Fair in Philadelphia. This world's fair of 1876, honored a century of American independence and celebrated the latest technology and design. Locomotives stood side-by-side with sewing machines, and buttons were displayed along with tractors and plows. The main exhibit buildings were iron structures with glass walls, overgrown greenhouses pointing the way to the steel and glass construction of the twentieth century, and following in the footsteps of the London Crystal Palace Exhibit of 1850. Individual countries built smaller buildings to represent their nation—and the British chose to construct a small "village" of three old-fashioned looking, charming domestic-scale buildings to showcase the new interest in the "artistic," that is, vaguely artisanal, or craftlike, architecture and arts.

Over eight million Americans came to see the Centennial during the five months it was open to the public. The same year as the Centennial, a group of Boston architects and publishers founded *The American Architect and Building News*. Reviews of the buildings of the Philadelphia Centennial Exposition filled several issues of the magazine in the first year of publication. Both the steel and glass exhibition halls and the smaller buildings representing each country were published as engravings and described in text, and the English exhibition buildings were particularly popular. The June 10, 1876 edition notes "The half-timbered houses of the British commission, in the style of two hundred years ago, have been so illustrated in *The Building News* and other papers that they must be familiar to our readers." But if the academic *American Architect and Building News* was new in that Centennial year, *The American Builder*, a trade publication, was an already established magazine with a readership of craftsmen and self-taught architect-builders. They also reviewed the British government's exhibit hall in Philadelphia.

> The chief thing that will strike the observant eye in this style is its wonderful adaptability to this country, not to the towns indeed, but to the land at large. It is to be hoped that the next millionaire who puts up a cottage at Long Branch will adopt this style, and he will have a house ample enough to entertain a Prince, yet exceedingly cozy, cool in summer and yet abundantly warm in winter, plain enough, and yet capable of the highest ornamental development.[3]

The British exhibition at the Centennial exhibit was not the first example of what we now identify as "Queen Anne style" architecture in the United States. That distinction goes to the Watts Sherman House, designed by Henry Hobson Richardson. Along with Richard Morris Hunt, H. H. Richardson was, for sheer talent and output, the pinnacle of American architecture in the post–Civil War era. Richardson is memorialized as the creator of "Richardsonian Romanesque" style, and he made only one real foray into the Queen Anne before he turned to the more substantial materials and forms of the Romanesque. However, his Watts Sherman House, built in 1874–1875, in Newport, Rhode Island, successfully incorporated many of the ideas present in Richard Norman Shaw's country houses. The Watts Sherman House uses multiple materials and a rambling, asymmetrical form held in check by a high, steep roof with a prominent front-facing gable, finished with half-timbering. The Watts Sherman House is a true landmark in American architecture, claimed as the forerunner of both the high-design Shingle Style and the vernacular-based Queen Anne style in domestic architecture. However stunning the

The British Building at the 1876 Centennial Exposition was the first example of the domestic designs based on historic English houses, like those being designed by Richard Norman Shaw, to be widely seen in the United States. The popularity of the British Building among American architects and the general public created a surge of imitators, thus forming the basis the American Queen Anne style.

"Leyswood," a country house designed by English architect Richard Norman Shaw in 1866, in rural Sussex, England, was published by the architectural press in the United States in the 1870s. This image is credited with introducing American designers to the Queen Anne style.

house, as the summer home of a wealthy family, the Watts Sherman House was of far less influence on the further development of either style than the less architecturally accomplished but much more visited houses at the Centennial Exhibition.

Stanford White, a young assistant in H. H. Richardson's office, is credited with much of the detailing of the Sherman house. Stanford White would become over the course of the next generation one of the most famous architects in the United States. Along with his partners, Charles F. McKim and William R. Mead, White took the English Queen Anne–style inspiration from Richardson and developed it into the Shingle Style. This sophisticated architectural form used the massing and informal plan first seen in the Watts Sherman House, with a tighter exterior surface, often made completely of wooden shingles. The Shingle Style was popular through the 1880s, particularly for resort-area architecture and suburban mansions. The sprawling plans and wooden cladding meant that the style was not suitable for urban or commercial construction, but it was in vogue among wealthy American clients for domestic architecture until another style, the Classical Revival, came along in the 1890s.

An image of the Watts Sherman House was circulated in another architectural publication, *The New York Sketch Book of Architecture*, in May 1875. Richard Norman Shaw, the leading English practitioner of Queen Anne domestic architecture, published his own work in a monograph in 1878, titled *Sketches for Cottages and Other Buildings*. This would have circulated to American architects and those with an interest in design. However, this would not have provided wide enough circulation to bring the image of the rambling Queen Anne house to a broader American consciousness. The imitators of Shaw's domestic work, and of the much-praised British House at the Centennial *did* seek to publish their latest designs. Indeed, there are dozens of drawings of houses that we would now identify as American Queen Anne from the first issues of *The American Architect and Building News*, although there are High Victorian Gothic examples and Stick Style and Shingle Style examples, too. None are labeled as to a style in the publication; they are presented as examples of "current work" of American architects, without comment. But *The American Architect and Building News* must share some of the credit for putting forth the images of new designs that came to be the American Queen Anne style, even as it came to decry the style in print.

The first American architectural press use of Queen Anne as a stylistic term for architecture appeared in June of 1876 in *The American Architect and Building News*. By December of that same year, the style is described in a not entirely flattering and complimentary manner in that magazine. The article credits Richard Norman Shaw with the "paternity" of the style, but questions what those buildings actually derive from the architecture of the original Queen Anne and her times. Then the writer goes in for the kill: "We need not mention any names, but the chief trouble with Mr. Shaw's Queen Anne occurs when it is done by other people." The author (identified at the end of the article only by the initial S) goes on to say of the Queen Anne, "It is a fashion of being old-fashioned...what is good is not Queen Anne and what is Queen Anne is not good; that it has no sort of validity or standing as a style; and that beginning as an attempt to re-establish a mere fashion which had gone irrevocably by, it is likely to end as a masquerade."[4]

The Watts Sherman House was the first example of a country house in the manner of Richard Norman Shaw built in the United States. Its early publication made it immensely influential in the development of the American Queen Anne style.

Thus, within one year of the start of its publication, the emerging voice of the American architectural establishment went on record as opposing the Queen Anne style. But the images it had published in that year, and would continue to publish without commentary in the next few years, ignited a taste for the picturesque buildings with elements of Old English, Tudor, Classical, Gothic, and other, more inventive, stylistic vocabularies all mixed together. Although the essays in *The American Architect and Building News* lauded the strict archaeological understanding of Gothic and Classical architecture, the magazine's pictures outweighed the closely spaced text in its impact on non-academic American builders and potential clients. *The American Architect and Building News* was the voice of the trained architect and building engineer, the artist and the college-educated man. It was not populist, and its critical stance was never intended to inform the majority of American builders. Thus, this quick reversal from interest to criticism of the Queen Anne style within its pages was never even noted by the American public, who responded favorably to the possibilities of the style as an expressive and comfortable model for modern domestic architecture.

The American Queen Anne style developed then as a vernacular architectural form, not as an academic one. During the 1880s and 1890s, the Academic architects dabbled with the Shingle Style for resorts and suburban houses, and then moved on to the Classical and Colonial Revival. But the architect-builders of America stayed with those first images of Queen Anne architecture, and worked to adapt them in American materials—chiefly wood and shingles—to create a recognizable and distinct American architecture. The willful irregularity of the exterior massing of a Queen Anne house allowed a great deal of informality and flexibility in the arrangement of interiors. This freedom from a formal plan was perhaps the most desirable element of all, expressing a new way of domestic living that valued function over form. The editorial staff of a tradesman's publication, *The Builder and Woodworker*, in 1880 acknowledged the twists and turns of the Queen Anne's adaptation to the American landscape; "We have been unable to find in any of the older text books any reference to the Queen Anne Style as now practiced. During the life of that esteemed lady (Queen Anne), the prevailing style of architecture was vastly different from that which now goes by her name."[5]

It was not the handful of trained architects practicing in urban areas who gave any of the Victorian styles their popularity in the United States. It was the authors of pattern books and the editors of the popular press, who often included articles on the latest architectural fashions for residences in farm magazines and the newly emerging "Lady's Books." Pattern books, beginning with those of Andrew Jackson Downing in the 1840s, aimed squarely at a middle-class audience, instilled in the reader the idea that a single-family, suburban house was the ideal to strive for. Unlike the earlier builder's books that showed the geometric "how-to" steps for building a staircase or detailing a mantelpiece, Downing presented illustrations of entire houses, with floor plans, and detailed advice on their architecture, siting, and decoration. Downing's first books were soon joined by those written by trained architects, experienced builders, architectural thinkers, and the occasional true eccentric. Not all found an audience; not all presented satisfying designs or practical advice, but as a phenomenon they increased exponentially the American public's knowledge of and interest in fashionable house building in the Victorian era.

The Queen Anne style was well promoted through pattern books by authors like William Comstock and Robert Shoppell, the Palliser Brothers, and George Barber. Their work was prescriptive, exhorting middle-class Americans with the virtues of home ownership, and the investment value of a well-designed home. The taste promoted in the pattern books after the Civil War turned increasingly "picturesque," to use the favorite word of the time, while everything else in the world became industrialized, including the printing processes that enabled pattern books to be cheaply produced and widely distributed by rail. The rise of the Industrial Revolution fostered among those who lived through its dramatic changes an appreciation of the increase in the availability of goods that made life easier, along with an acute awareness of the price paid for material prosperity. Water and air were polluted by factory discharge, industrial work was dangerous and mind-numbing, sprawling slums grew, and the rhythms of the seasons were replaced by the tyranny of the clock.

Nostalgia for the lost past, combined with enthusiasm for the future, colored the cultural perceptions of the United States in the nineteenth century. How else to explain the rise of the Hudson River School, glorifying grand natural landscapes, at the same moment many local streams and byways were being transformed to industrial sewers fed by mills? How else to understand the apparent tension between the historical, craft-based allusions of Queen Anne architecture with its mechanically produced decorations?

Queen Anne architecture could become a national vernacular style because the parts and pieces that made it were produced by machine. The turned porch posts, the latticework, the finials and cresting on rooflines, and the interior stairs and mantels were not the product of local woodworkers and a handcraft tradition. By the 1880s, specialty millwork shops used machines run by steam or even electricity to cut, turn, rout, and finish miles of woodwork for interior and exterior use. The manufacturers copied designs they saw in the architectural press, simplified sometimes to facilitate production. They put out catalogs of their goods, perhaps specializing in windows, porch posts, or doors. There was variation from each manufactory, but the overall output was remarkably similar. The catalogs repeated popular design first created by architect-builders, and then other builders and small-town architects used the ready-made architectural elements available through millwork catalogs, reinforcing the aesthetic and spreading it across the country.

Like most other domestic construction in the second half of the nineteenth century, the typical Queen Anne–style house would have been constructed using a "balloon frame." This in itself was an industrial, technological invention credited to Chicago builders of the 1830s, which was almost universally adopted in the United States by the time of the Civil War. The balloon frame used standard-size, industrially cut lumber nailed together in a lightweight wooden armature that defined the shape of a building and provided the attachment points for interior and exterior siding and finishes. Initially seen as "light as a balloon"—and hence the nickname, the balloon frame—this predecessor of today's similar platform framing of light, standardized-size lumber was a marked contrast to the older, heavy timber-framed construction methods.

As a contemporary builder noted, "… material is economized in these days of modern ideas and progress, the old principles, which were to use large timbers and cut them all to pieces by morticing [sic] and notching down to levels, being discarded and smaller timbers used, but so put together and constructed as to give greater strength without wasting material and labor." [6]

Balloon framing allowed a house frame to be constructed faster, and with a crew of less-skilled workmen than the joiners who had once made mortise-and-tenon joints for connecting huge, heavy timbers into a frame. Balloon framing also offered great freedom and ease in the construction of varied forms. A heavy timber frame goes together as a square or rectangular form. The balloon frame allowed more expressive plans and elevations, practically inviting construction of projecting bays and turrets, gables and cross-gables, all of which fit perfectly with the Queen Anne style.

The siding of Queen Anne–style houses most often includes a mix of textures or materials. Brick may cover the first floor, while wooden clapboards finish the second floor. Or a first floor may be clapboard, with shingles on the second floor and applied half-timber decoration in third-floor gables. This embodied the idea of the "picturesque" for the late-nineteenth-century homeowner, an attribute that could be further enhanced with multiple decorative windows, and a decorative treatment of the porch. *The American Architect and Building News* warned, "There is no need to copy old features merely because they are old, to strain after picturesqueness by placing, for instance,

Balloon framing, as shown in a pattern book of the late nineteenth century, allowed for more flexibility in the design and construction of a building than the traditional heavy-timber framing system. The many slender, small pieces of wood that formed the frame looked so light that many at the time thought the frame would blow away like a balloon.

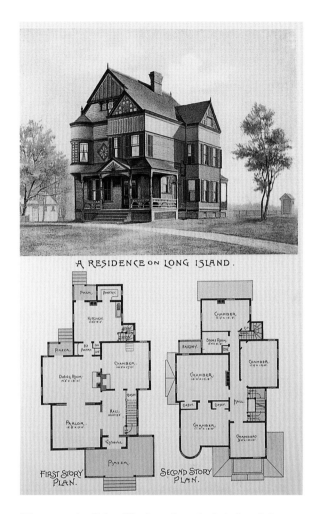

A RESIDENCE ON LONG ISLAND.

FIRST STORY PLAN. SECOND STORY PLAN.

The magazine Scientific American *included special editions on architecture in the 1880s through the early twentieth century, which were unique among the popular press for including color images. The pages of the magazine are one important source for understanding the role color played in Queen Anne houses.*

windows and fireplaces in most unsuitable positions. A style such as this cannot long survive."[7] But it did survive, in part because the new balloon framing allowed more flexibility in placing architectural elements; the position may have been "unsuitable" to an eye accustomed to symmetry on a façade, but in fact the freedom of the Queen Anne style allowed windows to appear on the exterior exactly where they were needed inside.

Another hallmark of the Queen Anne style was a new and daring use of color on the exterior, and the retreat from bright color on the interior. Ready-mixed paints became widely available about the time the style was introduced to America, revolutionizing the way paint was prepared, applied, and advertised. Paint is, first and foremost, a protective coating for wood or metal beneath it. Lead white, a paint prepared using tiny flakes of metallic lead mixed in linseed oil, had been known for thousands of years as an excellent protective coating. It was widely used in architectural finishes, and it could easily be tinted with other pigments to create a virtual rainbow of color.

Lead white pigment for paint was first commercially produced in the United States in 1815. Prior to that, it had been an expensive, imported commodity. White was immediately adopted as the color of choice for exteriors, and the choice fit the prevailing taste for classicism. As the Romantic Revival movement began to take hold in the 1830s and 40s, the new Gothic– and Italianate–style houses were painted in soft tones to blend with the landscape. Light yellows, pale grays, tans, pale olive-greens, and pinkish browns were preferred for the walls of such houses. As architectural eclecticism increased through the nineteenth century, bolder colors appeared. In addition, the tendency to highlight different parts of the building in different colors, that is, polychromatic treatments, on Gothic Revival and Stick Style houses, began in earnest after the Civil War period.

Not only was the use of more and richer color an aspect of changing fashion, there seems to have been a very practical aspect as well. As American factories, houses, schools, and churches began to consume coal for heating and the creation of electricity, the air above urban centers turned dirty and sooty. A white house would have turned gray in no time. The richer colors favored by the late nineteenth century were in some sense "protective coloration" in their environment.

As the inexpensive pattern books that transmitted so much information and advice about the Queen Anne style were all in black and white, there is frequently a description of the colors to be used for exteriors, and sometimes interiors. The emphasis on the use of multiple, rich colors in these written descriptions helps us to understand both the novelty of the palette and its direct association with the presentation of the architecture. For example, in the 1887 *Cottage Homes and Details* by George and Charles Palliser, they write of a rather modest two-story house, "The colors we suggest for painting the exterior are for first-story a maroon; shingle work of second story, terra cotta red; the panels in gables, etc., orange red; and the trimmings throughout, bronze green, the carved work on cornices, etc., being brought out with chrome yellow; window sash white and the outside blinds green of a lighter shade than the trimmings."[8]

The description above shows that poly-chromy—different colors on different parts of a building—was much in vogue at the time of the Queen Anne style. An article in the magazine, *Building*, in 1888, at the height of the style's popularity, was titled "The Decorative Use of Color." It noted that: "The use of polychromy for external decoration demands very careful attention; … In a building which has any pretense to architectural design, the polychromy of its structural features should be confined to that presented by its constructive materials"[9] In other words, each of the many materials or distinct design elements that made up the exterior decoration of the Queen Anne house should be emphasized with a different color.

The use of intense colors, with an emphasis on autumnal shades of reds, oranges, yellows, and bronze-greens, were the norm for the Queen Anne style. We have no color photographs from the period, but it was the beginning of the age of cheap color printing. While the inks were garish and none-too-subtle, many different sources of color print images from the end of the nineteenth century, including advertising, confirm that the palette from yellows to oranges to reds to browns was dominant on exteriors of the Queen Anne, and was used to "pick out" clapboard and shingles, as well as half-timbering and trim work.

An important contemporary source for color images of architecture was *Scientific American Architects and Builders Edition*. The venerable magazine of American science and invention, founded in 1846, published a special monthly edition from 1885 to 1905 showcasing domestic architecture. Houses were featured from around the country, in urban, suburban, and rural settings, but almost all were expressions of the Queen Anne style. The monthly "centerfold" was in color, showing the house in its setting, and accompanied by a floor plan, also in color. Red on the floor plan highlighted the presence of chimneys for decorative fireplaces and for the central heating stacks. Blue in the plans showed at a glance the presence of sinks and bathtubs, emphasizing the modernity of the houses.

SUPPLEMENT TO THE SCIENTIFIC AMERICAN-ARCHITECTS AND BUILDERS EDITION- JUNE 1886.

A HOUSE AT ORANGE, N.J.   JOSEPH A. STARK, ARCHITECT, NEW YORK.

The complex patterns and textures of even a modest Queen Anne style house were intended to be highlighted by the use of several different colors, typically in the shades of autumn. Oranges, reds, greens, browns, and golden-yellows were all popular for exteriors, while white, and cool colors like grays and blues were never used.

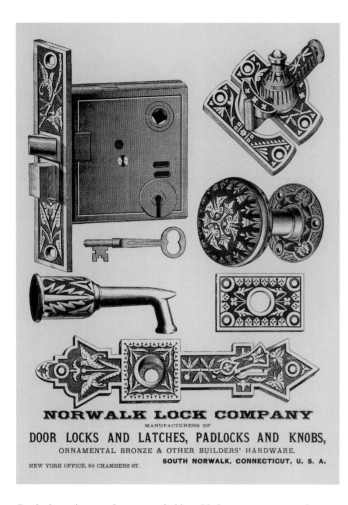

In the late nineteenth century, fashionable housewares were advertised in books and periodicals, and sold nationally. The improved transportation network in the United States gave formerly local companies of things like hardware and locks a national market, which contributed to the spread of a nationally recognizable style.

Scientific American, and advertising materials, particularly for paint companies, provides images of the rich colors of the Queen Anne style. The roofs were sometimes a solid gray slate, but more often a blue- or purple-hued slate, occasionally creating patterns with different colored slates. Outside of the cities, roofs were still very often wooden shingles, and painted an orange-red or dark green. The multiple textures and materials of the house would be highlighted with different colors—for the shingles, for the clapboard, for the corner boards, and for the strap work of false half-timbering. Wooden porches, balconies, verandas, and piazzas (all terms in common use at the time) might have their turned wooden members highlighted in another color. The window sash was yet another color, most often very dark, like a deep red or terra-cotta color, dark green, or black, and contrasted with the window trim surrounding the opening. Color was used boldly to accentuate materials and forms, and it became an important part of the Queen Anne house. Even simple houses used at least a three-color paint scheme. The house plans sold by mail through George Barber's 1890s publications included a color guide for outside painting; the Shoppell magazine-format house plan books included color-printed elevations of the featured house that could be cut out and glued together to create the model of the house, as it should be seen, in color.

One of the popular exterior colors of the Queen Anne, terra-cotta, was also a material of the same hue. Terra-cotta, the "baked earth" of ancient times, was revived as a manufactured architectural decoration, and widely used in domestic architecture in the latter nineteenth century. Terra-cotta could be molded and fired to create a long-lasting masonry element for a fraction of the cost of hand-carved stonework. Reddish-orange terra-cotta, matching the surrounding bricks, was used for decorative panels in chimneys even in relatively modest homes. In more elaborate houses, decorative terra-cotta panels provided rich, sculptural effects, such as bands of sinuous ornament under a cornice, or a curvaceous molded ridge along the top of the roof. Terra-cotta was used extensively and handsomely in urban buildings; in fact, the English Queen Anne Revival–style buildings were noted for their use of brick and terra-cotta.

The interest in rich exterior coloration extended to the choice of mortars binding together terra-cotta, or brick, or stone elements. Where masonry appeared on the Queen Anne building, it would almost never be white or light-toned, as in colonial times or as might be expected today. Instead, mortars were tinted with pigments, or colored sands, to produce mortar that either matched the surrounding brick and terra-cotta, or created a darker line between the masonry elements. Dark red and black mortars were common, and emphasized the uniformity of the masonry wall as a monolithic unit.

Terra-cotta was an exterior material, while its near-kin, tile, was used in the interior of the Queen Anne house. Tiles were used throughout the Victorian era, as their production became industrialized, making a former expensive handmade item widely available.

The 1884 book, *Manufacture of Bricks, Tiles and Terra-Cotta*, noted, "Nothing in the history of pottery is so remarkable as the progress which has been made in the manufacture of…decorative tiles…in this country since the Centennial Exposition of 1876."[10] Between 1870 and 1900, more than twenty-five companies producing floor and wall tiles opened in the United States, creating a domestic market for the material that was greatly increased by the aesthetic of the Queen Anne style.[11] The best tiles had been manufactured in England, but beginning in 1876, American firms began producing high-quality, beautiful "art tiles." In 1880, an American company, Low's Art Tiles, took the gold medal in an international competition held near Stoke-on-Trent, the traditional center of the English ceramic industry. Low's Art Tiles and the many American firms that arose to imitate them, suddenly made high-quality tile available to the American domestic market. Many of these art tiles of the last quarter of the nineteenth century included sculptural relief decorations, illustrating figures of myth or sentimental charm, in soft colors. Many of these art tiles were destined for highlighting fireplace surrounds in Queen Anne–style houses. Other tiles were used to cover the walls or bathrooms and kitchens, where the easy-to-clean and sanitary qualities of the material made it a popular choice. In some houses, vestibules or entries had floors of tile. The American machine-made tile was inexpensive compared to the highly expensive imported handmade tiles of just a half century before, and so tiles were another material embraced in the middle-class home as newly accessible, with the added benefit of great durability and utility in places where water would often be a consideration.

Tiles tend to survive in Queen Anne houses, as integral parts of the building, in a way that other decorative elements—paint color, wallpaper, or plumbing fixtures—did not. In their original setting, the tiles were part of the whole effect of interiors with patterned wallpapers, patterned carpets, textured sheer curtains underneath patterned drapes, and richly colored, patterned upholstered furnishings.

The appeal of the Queen Anne house was far more than its applied decoration, however, much as the critics liked to target that aspect. The visible style was a product of the industrial age, in the variety of materials available, and their factory-made designs. Inside, Queen Anne houses were also industrial to their core. The era of the Queen Anne house—from 1876 to 1900—marks the period when many modern inventions related to daily life were developed, and American domestic architecture universally incorporated this technology.

A popular builder and promoter of Queen Anne–style houses wrote in 1887: "There is springing up a National Style which is becoming more distinctive in character and unlike that of any other nation, as the American climate, life, economy [is distinctive]… requiring greater facilities and conveniences with snug and comfortable quarters for Winter and shady porches and verandas for Summer."[12] The builder-author recognized that Americans wanted their domestic designs with a big dose of comfort, a trend that shows no signs of abating in today's home-building market.

The pattern-book author S. B. Reed summed up the technological improvements of the Queen Anne house when he wrote in his 1885 book *Dwellings for Village and Country*:

> If we compare dwellings of the average class erected within the past two years, with those built thirty, twenty or even ten years ago, we discover marked differences in their arrangement, style and construction….Cellars are of less depth in the earth, with increased elevations of foundations above the ground, insuring more airy basements with much healthier living apartments above. Higher ceilings are given.…heating by furnaces, insuring uniform temperature throughout; systems of ventilation; introduction of water with perfect methods of distribution of both cold and hot water; bath and wash tubs, water closets, gas pipes, drainage, dumb waiters, bells, speaking tubes, burgular [*sic*] alarms, lightning conductors, improved hardware, etc. etc. None of these things are found in the dwellings of the "olden time." Now all these can be had at little cost, and are more or less included in our newer dwellings. Less house work and more comfort is the result.[13]

As early as 1873, the British magazine *The Builder*, was running articles like "Health and Comfort in House Building," which advocated above all, ventilation, through mechanical devices to regulate air intake and discharge throughout a house. The article also emphasized the need for windows to provide light and views that were "cheerful, lively and interesting."[14] Ventilation and windows, famously summed up as "sweetness and light" came to be a characteristic of Queen Anne architecture in England and also in America. During the "Victorian" era, the technology of glass production allowed for larger individual sheets of glass and the reduction in the number of surface impurities.[15] Plate glass appeared as early as the 1830s in commercial and civic buildings; by the 1850s it was being used in expensive, high-style houses, and by the 1880s it was advertised for use in American Queen Anne–style houses.

The technology for making glass had been improved and industrialized in the nineteenth century, and the ability to make ever-larger panes of glass was encouraged by the use of larger expanses of uninterrupted glass in architectural designs. In colonial America, when "large" panes of glass were often no more than 8 x 10 inches, a window had to be composed of many small panes of glass held together in wooden muntins. The muntin evolution of nineteenth-century America—from 6/6 sash in the Federal period to the common 2/2 sash of the post–Civil War period—indicates the ability of American manufacturers to produce consistently larger sheets of glass at an affordable price, which required less wood in the way of muntins, to compose a large window. Large windows, uninterrupted by muntins were unknown before the latter nineteenth century, and hence were embraced by the public as they became available. Only with the conscious historicism of the Queen Anne style, which tried to recall the quaint picturesqueness of the past, were small windowpanes back in fashion. But only to a point. The classic Queen Anne window of the 1880s and 90s in American domestic architecture is an upper sash outlined with small panes, the muntins creating a sort of frame around a larger pane of glass in the center. The lower sash was typically undivided by muntins. Thus a decorative show of small old-fashioned windows was expressed without compromising the desirable "modern" aesthetic of uninterrupted glass.

Indeed, one of the arguments put forth by academic architects against the Queen Anne style was precisely about windows. At the February 1877 monthly meeting of the Boston Society of Architects, those assembled discussed the Queen Anne style. One person present said, "It is a style which requires of the architect of to-day the sacrifice of many modern notions which have come to be regarded as indispensable, such as large sheets of plate glass, double hung sash, narrow house-lots in cities, etc." This point was countered by Mr. Van Brunt, the president of the Society and a noted architect, who observed, "The interior features of the style are extremely interesting and quite adapted to modern uses."[16]

A Richard Norman Shaw commercial building constructed in London in 1872 was lavishly praised in the English architectural press for being "unusually light and well ventilated." Shaw was praised by the critics not for the design itself but for "the favor with which the building is viewed arises from having good access to all parts, and the care bestowed by the architect on the provision of light and air."[17]

Glass was also colored, beveled, and etched, using light as part of the decoration of interiors. Stained glass, formerly only associated with ecclesiastical buildings, moved

The Queen Anne style promoted distinctive windows, with complex patterns in the upper sash and large, open panes of glass in the lower sash. The small panes provided the "antique" look for the historical precedents of the style while the large piece of glass acknowledged the modernity of the building.

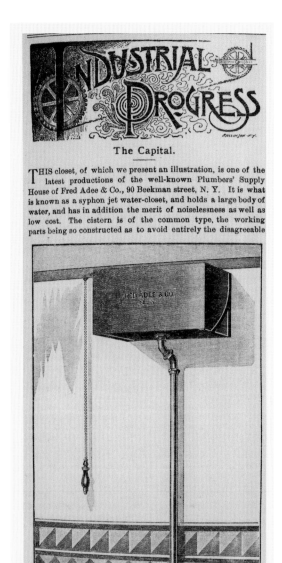

One of the constant concerns of architects, builders, and homeowners during the late nineteenth century was sanitation. This illustration of a water closet from 1891 shows the delight in form and function that such domestic improvements sparked.

into domestic architecture to a limited extent in the mid-nineteenth century with the Gothic Revival style. As with so many other building elements, industrial production and falling prices made stained glass accessible as a decorative feature for a wide range of homebuilders, and it was widely adopted as at least an accent feature in many buildings. Most typically, stained glass was placed near an entry or over the staircase. In the best Queen Anne houses, where a large entry hall contained the main staircase, stained glass almost always made an appearance. The stained glass in most domestic uses was not figurative, but floral, foliate, or abstract designs, sometimes customized to include the owner's initials or emblem of the family's work and associations. Beveled-edge plate glass began to be used commonly in the large windows set in the upper portion of exterior doors, using the exterior door as an added light source for the interior. Etching glass was another way to add unique decorative effects, and offered a chance for diffuse light while obscuring direct views. Etched glass with motifs of ferns or birds was particularly popular for front entrances.

In addition to light, "sweetness" or the freshness of air was of paramount concern. Unlike the eighteenth century, which shunned the night air, the nineteenth century celebrated the therapeutic powers of fresh air at all hours of the day or night. Resort communities advertised their virtues on the promises of "fresh air" and scenery, whether they were located near the ocean or the mountains.

From 1870 to 1876, a series of inventions and patents brought forth the flushable, vented, ceramic toilet, which sweetened the domestic scene considerably. The discovery of germ theory and its broad acceptance across America and Western Europe led to an unprecedented period of public works construction designed to isolate a clean water supply and deliver it efficiently to urban populations. By the 1880s, public sewage systems in major cities were under construction. The new Queen Anne house was connected to a larger municipal system of waste-water management that eliminated odors and unsanitary conditions near the home; the discovery of venting by pipe the plumbing system of a building to equalize pressure and siphon off odors opened the way for innovation in toilet design and construction. Similarly, the removal of waste from cities was changed from street runoff to sewage and drainage pipes out of sight and out of smell from the general population.

Wealthy Americans had long tried various mechanisms for indoor facilities through the nineteenth century; for instance, Thomas

Jefferson devised an indoor privy at his home in Monticello, but it required slaves to haul away the filled chamber pots and refill the wood ashes under the wooden seat. The Tremont Hotel in Boston, constructed in 1829 and designed by Isaiah Rogers, set the standard for a modern, first-class hotel and it included water closets on the ground floor and rooms for bathing in the basement. It sounds crude today, but in eliminating an outdoor walk to the privy and offering private bathing, the Tremont advanced the comfort expectations of thousands of hotel guests. In the mid-nineteenth century, wealthy homebuilders included lead- or zinc-lined water storage tanks in the attics. Water was pumped up to the tank by a hand- or wind-driven machine, and then fed by gravity into pipes leading to sinks and basins. Obviously there was no temperature control possible in this system. Only when municipal water systems were developed, which supplied water under sufficient pressure to allow it to rise up into a house, could it be passed through a heating device to permit warm water to come out of the taps.

During the 1870s and 80s, more and more houses were constructed as extensions of this drive for municipal sanitation. When the architectural press was not debating the merits of style, they were promoting advances in municipal and individual sanitation. The invention of the reliable cast-ceramic flush toilet was heralded in the 1870s, and its successful commercial production in America was pursued by several inventors and manufacturers. A series of articles appeared in the American periodical *Architecture and Building* in the fall of 1892, entitled "The Victorian Era, the Age of Sanitation." Truly, the era of Queen Victoria's reign from 1837 to 1901 produced deep changes in the concept and technology of sanitation, many of which found direct expression in the design of Queen Anne houses.

So it was largely the architects and builders of the Queen Anne style, working in the same era as the perfection of indoor plumbing, who established the aesthetic of the modern bathroom. They decided early on that ceramic finishes were more sanitary than wood in a room where water was a constant. So for over a century, the bathroom was the one room consistently finished with tile while other rooms in an American house were not. The Queen Anne house incorporated all the plumbing fixtures—toilet, tub, and sink—into one room and there they have remained in modern American houses; but Europeans more commonly separate bathing facilities from the toilet.

The very early pattern books present designs and plans for houses in the last quarter of the nineteenth century, such as George and Charles Palliser's *Model Homes* of 1878, include a variety of small rural cottages, urban row houses, and freestanding suburban dwellings. Most of the illustrations in this pattern book are not Queen Anne in style, but a late Gothic Revival–Stick Style combination. The smallest cottages do not show indoor plumbing incorporated, but the urban row houses, even when small and inexpensive, will include a "water closet," often set on the first floor or even in the basement. Suburban houses are about evenly split as to whether they include a full bathroom, a water closet alone, or no indoor facilities.

A decade later, the brothers Palliser again published a book of house designs. *New Cottage Homes and Details*, published in 1887, is filled with houses squarely in the Queen Anne style. Just over two hundred designs and plans for houses are shown, and about one-quarter of them are designed without bathrooms and water closets. These are usually explicitly noted in the accompanying text as houses for the country, where presumably there is space on the property for a privy and enough distance between the privy and the water supply for the house. Most commonly the bathroom is now located on the second floor, near the bedrooms. The bedrooms themselves in this period now all have individual closets, another mark of modernity in the Queen Anne house. It is perhaps a reflection of the material prosperity that contributes to the varied appearance of the style that closets to store an excess of goods are required in middle-class American homes, a situation without precedent in earlier historical times.

The last great popularizer of the Queen Anne style, George Barber, who published two books of architectural plans that were sold nationally in the 1890s, included bathrooms in the plans for almost all of his houses, even the smallest cottages. A few houses contained "bath rooms" with a tub for bathing, but no indoor toilet. Barber recommended in his preface to one pattern book that where possible, homebuilders consider including a bedroom with attached bathroom on the first floor of the house, to accommodate the elderly and invalids.[18]

And while the number of houses with indoor plumbing had steadily increased during the period of the Queen Anne, the topic was still new enough that an 1893 publication entitled *Suburban and Country Homes* devoted five and a half pages to general "Suggestions on House Building" and eight full pages on "How to Plumb a Suburban House." It was not really detailed enough to make it a "how-to" for the builder or plumber, but it did explain how systems worked, what materials were needed, and sample specifications from the construction of a house. The intended audience was clearly the potential homebuilder, who would be convinced to spend extra money to incorporate water closets and bathtub, slop and laundry sinks, and kitchen sink, all connected to pipes of iron or brass, as appropriate.[19]

Plumbing was not only used for sanitary systems, but also for steam and hot-water heating, two of the most common methods of home heating in the latter part of the nineteenth century. Central heating was introduced in America as early as 1800 in the homes of a very few rich people. Early heating systems required as much manpower as mechanical power to operate vents, keep a furnace stoked, and regulate the heat. But by the time of the Civil War, boilers and furnaces were a common item, and they moved from powering factories to heating homes about 1880. The Queen Anne house almost always included a fireplace, but as a symbolic hearth and not as the primary source of heating. Furnaces were in the basement, and the heat generated there from the burning of (most commonly) coal brought heat into the house through two methods. The first used the simple principle that heat rises, and warm air was brought into living spaces through floor grates or "registers." The other main method of distributing central heating was to bring water to a boil in the furnace, and allow the steam to travel through pipes into the main rooms via radiators. In 1881, the American Radiator Company patented a cast-iron radiator that was useful and affordable for domestic installations. Both methods left some rooms toasty and others chill, but they were a vast improvement over the rudimentary central heating systems in use prior to the 1880s. Although the coal that powered the furnace was dirty, it was confined to a "coal cellar" and the house itself remained clean, without the soot common to iron stoves and fireplaces, which had caused endless toil for housewives and servants of earlier generations.

Cleaner energy was on the way in the 1880s, but it would be another half century before American homes were consistently heated with something other than coal. But lighting was greatly improved in the Queen Anne house

Furnaces, and the apparatus of central heating, including radiators and thermostats, first made their appearance for the domestic market during the period the Queen Anne house was popular. The Queen Anne house was markedly cleaner, and more comfortable, than previous generations of houses, for having a basement furnace instead of room-by-room fireplaces or stoves for heating.

thanks to the widespread availability of, first, pressurized natural gas, and then, electricity. Gas, for lighting, was first used for public streets in the United States in Baltimore as early as 1816. It was introduced into business and residences through the nineteenth century, and it was widely available, at least in urban locations, following the Civil War. Out in rural America, where indeed most of the nation still lived, Queen Anne–style houses might have relied on even older lighting sources, like kerosene lamps. Edison's light bulb, invented in 1879, was only useful if electricity was widely available to power it. Edison himself ordered the construction of power plants (often coal-fired in the urbanized East) and the organization of public utilities to provide and deliver electricity to the consumer. There are many houses from the 1880s and 90s that show the lack of reliable systems of electricity, in the installation of dual fixtures, served by both gas and electric. If one system went out, the other would take over.

As pattern-book author George Barber wrote in 1896, "It has been our aim, by the means of this work, to present to the home-builder something attractive in exterior design, combined with conventional, practical interior arrangement that can not but be helpful for those desiring to build."[20] The combination of design with functionality has always been a precept of architecture, but in the American Queen Anne style it reached a fever-pitch of innovation for both. Queen Anne Houses are "absurdities...piled up without rhyme or reason—restless, turreted, gabled, loaded with meaningless detail, defaced with fantastic windows and hideous chimneys…the more "features" a house has, the more "artistic" it is considered."[21] The source of this particular criticism was a landscape artist, Ernest Piexotto. He sketched architecture for some of the leading publications of the late nineteenth century, and from there it was an easy step to architectural criticism. He reflects the point of view of the elite, the established academic; and while he derides the term "artistic," it was indeed rising in popularity with the Queen Anne style.

By the late 1880s and 1890s, the Queen Anne house was known as an "artistic" design and sometimes referred to in the popular press as "the National Style." George Palliser, pattern-book author and promoter noted "It would be folly for us, who live in the nineteenth century, [in] a nation noted for its inventive genius, to undertake to transplant to this new country any foreign style which was perfected centuries ago, and which, though eminently fitted for the age in which it flourished, is not adapted to our wants and times…" Although historicism was the starting point, the Queen Anne house advanced as a unique and modern expression of material prosperity and technological ingenuity.

"Whatever may be said by architects, to the ordinary city man the building of these cottages (in the Queen Anne style) began what was a cheering and pleasing relief…spots where the new style began to show itself were visited as the parks used to be, and a new and lasting interest was aroused in suburban homes. The fad may have gone too far for a time, and it may be true that there are houses of a style of architecture which can only be classed with the miscellaneous, but nevertheless, as compared to the houses that used to be built, a certain number to the block and all of the same style, like so many blocks of wood cut off to order from the same log, they were a great improvement in the eyes of the home seeker of moderate means."[22]

And there is the contemporary summation—Queen Anne houses were immensely popular with real estate developers, with community members for increasing the variety and beauty of residential streets, and with homebuilders and homebuyers and their children and grandchildren, down to those of us who live in and love Queen Anne houses today. The Queen Anne house does appear nationally—even in Alaska and Hawaii— and it is always charming for its individuality, for a free spatial layout that provides unexpected nooks and crannies, and for a confident expression of the love of materials. The development of the Queen Anne style is the triumph of popular taste over the academic, and in many ways, the creation of a national vernacular style that is uniquely identifiable as American. Is there any style that did not have examples that "went too far" and inappropriately subverted its designs? But "too far" is in the eye of the beholder, and in the pages that follow, there are many examples of Queen Anne houses that have been loved by generations, preserved and cared for in all their idiosyncratic glory. ✸

INTERIOR DECORATION

The American Queen Anne interior is the quintessential expression of abundance and layering. Yet it has its intellectual roots in the notion that art should express simplicity and "honesty" in materials and design. These attributes first came to the fore with the English designers of the latter nineteenth century now known for creating the "Arts and Crafts" movement. The Arts and Crafts movement at first began with medieval sources and the preindustrial work of earlier centuries as inspiration for honest design. Handcrafted work and beautiful art designs were produced, but they were so expensive as to be out of reach of most people.

When Arts and Crafts ideals were harnessed to mass production in order to create affordable and saleable items for interior decoration, the result was neither particularly medieval nor artistically honest. The popular movement to transform handmade medieval design into mass-produced material goods was christened "The Aesthetic Movement," and it soon embraced a wide range of design sources. General taste in America and England moved quickly away from strictly medieval forms, due, in no small measure, to the fact that life in the nineteenth century involved more and varied forms of furnishing and decoration than ever were available in earlier centuries. Medieval source material was too limited to provide credible designs for the upholstered sofas and chairs, floor coverings and wallpapers that the modern public wanted.

The American Architect and Building News article on the British pavilion at the 1876 Centennial Exhibition included this description of that prototype for American Queen Anne design: "The interior is pleasantly fitted up with staircases, mantels, and furniture of dark oak, wainscoting, and rich sober-hued paper-hangings. A singular

Gathered around the piano, the ladies are surrounded by multi-patterned wallpaper, lace-edged furniture scarf, a decorative vase, and family photographs. All these were hallmarks of the proper and well-decorated middle-class interior in the Queen Anne style.

effect is produced by painting the wainscoting a dark dull chocolate brown, with ebonized beading, which is rather gloomy in itself but combines well with the wallpapers of the style now in vogue in England, with brown, blue-greens, and neutral grounds relieved by dull red and gold. The ceilings in the lower story are papered in white, buff and gold. The whole effect is quite rich."[23]

The richness of the Aesthetic Movement that translated to the vernacular American Queen Anne interior was, to a considerable degree, a testimony to the ability of goods to be mass-produced and made available at a much lower cost than ever before. It was the look of "rich," albeit largely "nouveaux riches" (the term was coined during the Gilded Age, which was coincident with the ascendancy of the Queen Anne style), that was the overwhelming choice of American homeowners in the late nineteenth century. So many decorative items, formerly handmade and expensive, were being produced by machine at all quality levels and prices. If two generations before, an American family only owned what they or their neighbors could produce, what temptation then to include formerly inaccessible items like wallpaper, tapestry, velvet drapes, inlaid wood, ceramic vases, tiles, and silk-braid tassels? In our own time, familiarity with and accessibility to all these things and more have laid down rules of "taste" that declare this is all too much! But it is unfair to judge the Queen Anne interior by our own standards, and far more useful to see it not as a symptom of bad taste, but as the exuberant expression of the machine age, newly exulting in the availability of goods, and a delight in their material and variety.

The resulting interiors seemed restless and over-full, and this was recognized even by contemporaries. A review of an 1877 book on interior decoration by the English architect J. M. Talbert noted that in the designs: "No space or point capable of receiving a decoration is neglected; and the result is, in several of these compositions, a want of subordination of parts, and consequently of repose and true elegance."[24]

Another commentator of the time wrote, "And so it goes through all interior decoration…sunflowers, sconces, blue china, turned work instead of notches and chamfers, and above all Japanese screens, fans, stuffs, papers, pictures, bronzes, china…. In our judgment of it we greatly err in calling it 'Queen Anne' for that after all is but one little phase of a strong reaction… On the contrary, all this can only truly be thought of as the period of odds and ends, beauty in any form, cosiness, comfort, picturesqueness,—in short, the 'bric-a'-brac' style."[25]

Just as drawings of house plans and elevations were presented by the architectural press in America, so, too, were designs for Queen Anne interiors published beginning in the 1870s. More general magazines also took up the interest in fashionable decorating, so that all manner of cheap, widely available printed materials, complete with black and white illustrations, were available to an American audience to show them what was new.

Popular books of the early 1880s included pattern-book author Robert Shoppell's *How to Build, Furnish and Decorate*, and William B. Tuthill's *Interiors and Interior Design*. Both illustrated interior decoration in the Queen Anne style for a popular audience.[26]

Two other books were widely influential in bringing a narrative of the ideas of the Aesthetic Movement interior to a broad American public. The first was *Hints on Household Taste*, by English decorator Charles Eastlake, first published in 1868 in London. Eastlake's book was so influential, his name is now often used synonymously with Aesthetic Movement design. The book went to several editions; the 1878 version, with new and improved illustrations, particularly captured American fancy. It also was well-timed to appeal to an audience who had seen and appreciated the Aesthetic interiors of the British Pavilion at the 1876 Centennial Exhibition, and desired to learn more about how to recreate such a look in their own homes.

As Eastlake himself wrote in *Hints on Household Taste*, "Artistic taste in the nineteenth century, based as it is upon eclecticism rather than on tradition, is capricious and subject to constant variation." His book takes a room-by-room approach to the house, recommending certain pieces of furniture, as well as the appropriate floor coverings, window treatments, and so on, down to the accessories like mirrors and vases.

The frontispiece for Clarence Cook's The House Beautiful *shows the ideal woman in the ideal house, doing her domestic duties.*

Eastlake extols handcrafted, medieval-inspired elements, but recognizes that most households were unlikely to find or afford such items, and so he does include a nod to modern manufacturing with notes on who produces the best electro-plated silverware or imitation crystal. Because the book is English in origin, its helpful information on sources—the shops and craftsmen in and around London who made and sold the wares he described—was of little use to an American audience.

This was rectified beginning in 1875, when Clarence Cook, an American journalist and art critic, began a series of articles in the popular *Scribner's Monthly* magazine on the decorative dictums of the Aesthetic Movement. The last of the articles was published in May 1877, and in 1882, they were reworked and combined into a book titled *The House Beautiful*. Cook was strongly influenced by Eastlake's book, dividing his into the same type of chapters dealing with different rooms, and sprinkling illustrations of particular pieces of furniture throughout, just as Eastlake had done.

As Cook wrote, however, "I have no mission to preach a crusade against luxury and bad taste; nor have I a hope that anything I can say will bring back simplicity and good taste…simplicity seems to me a good part of beauty, and utility only beauty in a mask; and I have no prouder nor more pretending aim than to suggest how this truth my be expressed in the furniture and decoration of our homes."[27] Cook then goes on for more than

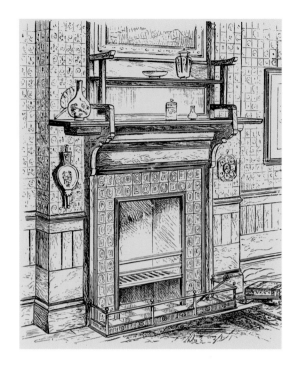

three hundred pages to write about details that go well beyond simplicity and utility, and the book illustrates several very costly pieces of furniture. But Clarence Cook's *House Beautiful* carried a distinctive American stamp, for it favored early colonial antiques over European medieval ones, and did preach—yes, that is the only word to describe his moralizing tone—the virtues of having an "inner life" of value over the mere acquisition of things.

Cook was a great and constant champion of early American arts, at a time when European work was generally favored for decorative arts and architecture. Cook's interior-design advice gave a boost to the Colonial Revival movement then just beginning. He even mentioned "Mr. McKim, one of the foremost of our young architects"[28] for his "restoration" (the quotation marks are Cook's and would be supported by restoration architects today) of an old house in Newport, Rhode Island. The *House Beautiful* supported the first appreciation of American colonial decorative arts, and may be said to have created the market for American antiques.

The fireplace, while no longer needed for heating the house, remained an important center for decoration, as shown in this illustration from The House Beautiful.

If the integration of American colonial design elements with Aesthetic-movement furniture was the core of interior decoration in the Queen Anne period, it was enriched further by incorporation of personal mementos as a part of public display. As noted in the magazine *Building*, "The domestic interior, in which picturesque arrangement, suggestions of historical association or foreign travel, or the collector's taste, may often play a more important part than either architecture or decorative color."[29] The "curio cabinet" was developed for domestic use during this period, to house things that were collected and displayed, communicating the homeowner's education, aesthetic aspirations, or travel. The display of souvenirs from other contemporary cultures, particularly Asian and Native American, were matched with antiques from American and European sources. All were uniformly considered exotic, and often were put together in an eclectic mix in a homeowner's curio cabinet or displayed on the mantel. The results of such mix-and-match were considered "picturesque" and therefore met the highest standard of aesthetic judgment for the period.

The Queen Anne interior focused on the "living hall"—a central space intended to recall the medieval "hall" where dining and social spaces were combined. However, in nineteenth-century America, there was no interest in one-room living. The ceremonial aspects of the medieval hall were retained, but it was typically less a room for lingering within than a space to pass through to other, specialized rooms, including the dining room and parlors. A Queen Anne house's "living hall" usually included the main staircase, often a fireplace for atmosphere and as an area of display, and, occasionally, enough space for some sort of a seating area. Unlike the straight, narrow center halls of earlier houses, the ideal living hall of a Queen Anne house included natural light sources and a spatial configuration that was more roomlike in dimension.

Clarence Cook encouraged homeowners to eschew symmetry in domestic arrangement, and to avoid the matched suites of furniture. He wrote, "Nature, who never makes two sides of a leaf alike, nor two sides or a flower…will surely repay industrious study of her works by some hint of how not to do it, when we are bent on seeing our back parlor reflected in our front one like the sky in a mill-pond." He goes on, "Each room ought to be considered by itself, no matter if it be only nominally separated from another by the piers on each side of a wide arch-way. Its floor, its walls, its ceilings out [*sic*] to be brought into harmony by a right arrangement of color—that is the first thing."[30]

The House Beautiful explained to its readers that one way to arrange color was to allow the wall to be divided up into "its natural parts," as Cook saw it, with wainscot, main wall area, and frieze area. Each area could use its own pattern or hue, but Cook hoped that the patterns and color were in harmony, and made "an agreeable impression upon the eye."[31]

Then there was the ceiling, which "ought to be married to the wall by being papered or painted in harmony with it." He continued this line of thought: "There is no reason at all why a ceiling should not be papered as well as a wall…[and] the paper on the wall should not be repeated on the ceiling." With wallpaper patterns on walls and ceiling, and perhaps distinctively different papers on different areas of the wall, it is not surprising that later designers saw the Queen Anne interior as a terribly distracting clash of color and pattern. It is interesting to note that the English *Hints on Household Taste* does not advocate ceiling papers, and in fact admonishes; "Paperhangings should in no case be allowed to cover the whole space of a wall from skirting to ceiling."[32]

This shows that the American Queen Anne interior was, if anything, more exuberant than the English originals, and constitutes an independent aesthetic development, just as the American Queen Anne style of architecture represents a unique and vigorous departure from British creations. 🐚

LEFT: *This interior illustration of a typical Queen Anne stair hall was published in* The American Architect and Building News *in 1880.*

RIGHT: *Even without color printing, the black and white illustrations of the era's popular decorating guides gave a clear idea of the complexity of pattern and design that characterized the Queen Anne–style interior.*

SUMMER HOUSES

SUMMER HOUSES HAVE a long history of being the place for architectural innovation. A new idea from an architect may have a difficult time being made into brick and mortar in an expensive urban location, or close to the scrutiny of one's boss or opinionated acquaintances. But a summer house seems to allow a relaxation of expectations, just as the summer vacation itself does. The owner of a summer house clearly has substantial financial means, and will not be dismissed by a judgmental world on the basis of the appearance of a summmer house alone. A year-round residence is the place for serious expression and ostentation, if that is desired. The summer house is a place for experimentation, for freedom from the routine and the expected, and thus for trying out a new style.

The Queen Anne style of architecture was formed in the United States in Newport, Rhode Island, among the summer houses of the very wealthy. From the experiments there in the mid-1870s, there developed both the Shingle Style of architecture and the Queen Anne. The Shingle Style remained high-brow and largely the province of architects; the Queen Anne merged with the vernacular building tradition of American carpenters and builders to form a new, national style.

The summer houses that follow include three from Newport, Rhode Island. Each illustrates some aspect of the Queen Anne style's development. The seminal Watts Sherman House created the vocabulary and a form for Queen Anne houses so perfect that every house in the style that follows contains some echo of it. Castle Hill, designed and built by an unknown architect-builder, but an assured creation nonetheless, illustrates how the Queen Anne style was easily transferred to the vernacular builders because it used a familiar material, wood, along with the unfamiliar details. The Charles Baldwin House was published nationally even before construction was complete, both validating its appearance and providing a model for at least parts of many more houses across America.

Two other summer houses are included. Theodore Roosevelt's Sagamore Hill in Long Island and the Edward Brooke House in Pennsylvania were built a decade after those first examples in Newport, and illustrate the full maturation of the Queen Anne style. Both examples were designed by architects of some renown, both in their own day and in ours. The Queen Anne style was lambasted by the architectural press but the extreme flexibility presented by its open floor plans and the possibilities for personalization of the decoration made it irresistible as a summer house expression.

Changing tastes and changing technology often render buildings fashionable or obsolete, but because of its expense and its collaborative nature, the art of architecture can take a long time to become the habitable building of a client's dream. The best dreams start on a lazy summer's day…

WATTS SHERMAN HOUSE, NEWPORT, RHODE ISLAND

THE BROAD FRONT GABLE, shingle siding at the second floor, and stone base firmly rooting the house to the landscape have become familiar and accepted visual elements of American domestic architecture, as a result of its frequent expression during the late nineteenth century. Likewise, it is unremarkable to see grouped windows with multiple panes on one sash, over a single large sash beneath. Medievalizing details like paneled chimneys and decorated bargeboards are known on many houses of the latter nineteenth century. But where they all appeared first, together, was in the Watts Sherman House in Newport, Rhode Island; thus it is this house which carries the title of the originator of the Queen Anne style in the United States.

The house is named for William Watts Sherman (1842–1912), a physician by training, banker by trade, and the son of a wealthy family. And in 1871, he was also the lucky groom of Annie Derby Rogers Wetmore (1848–1884), from an extremely prominent family in Newport. The Shermans had the house built in 1874–75, on property given to Mrs. Sherman by her father, who had his own summer place next door. The well-educated and well-traveled couple sought out the most lauded architect in America at that moment to design their new home. Henry Hobson Richardson (1838–1886) had just completed Trinity Church in Boston, a modern masterpiece utilizing the Romanesque style as its inspiration. The solidity and ancient qualities of that style were very much on his mind when the Shermans' commission for a summer house came in to his office. But Richardson's Romanesque vision was also overlaid with images he had seen of country houses in England by architect Richard Norman Shaw (1831–1912). Shaw's "manor houses" adopted the architectural vocabulary of vernacular English country houses of the late seventeenth and early eighteenth centuries, and combined them into picturesque new structures.

The rusticated stone base of dark stone is not the obvious choice for a summer house by the coast, but it anchors a light wooden structure on the second floors and in attic gables, finished with shingles and pierced by many windows. The balance of light and dark, solid and weightless, vertical (for the house is quite tall) and horizontal (the dominant expressive line of the building) makes the Sherman House such a brilliant design. Richardson's great innovation was to include the medieval-inspired decorative details, popularized by contemporary English architect Richard Norman Shaw, with an innovative plan that allowed rooms to flow freely from one into the other.

Richardson's Watts Sherman House was, in fact, such a perfect summary of modern (for the time) domestic architecture that he never sought to develop it further. Richardson continued to work in the Romanesque style, and on civic and ecclesiastical commissions, but he never returned to the Shavian manor house in any of his commissions. That architectural development was left to a very young, and very talented draftsman, Stanford White (1853–1906), who worked in Richardson's office from 1872–78. White is credited with much of the detailing of the original Watts Sherman House, and drawings in his hand for details survive. White went on to make up one-third of the seminal American architectural firm, McKim, Mead and White, who developed the full-blown Shingle Style in the 1880s.

The Watts Sherman house was published in a small, short-lived periodical, *The New York Sketch Book of Architecture* in 1876. But because it was published in New York, and at the same time as the popular Centennial Exhibition in Philadelphia showcased the British government's "Queen Anne" style house,

the Watts Sherman House drew widespread attention from American architects and builders. The intricate details of the drawing of the Sherman House pointed the way for thousands of variations, something no architect or builder could resist, and offered a way to create new and practical floor plans that broke out of the traditional rectangular box with narrow halls and distinct rooms that had defined most high-style houses up to that time.

The Watts Sherman House was built only for summer use in Newport, Rhode Island. Originally conceived as a "cottage," it was a rather simple rectangular-shaped house under a high, steep roof enlivened with gables. The main level had a broad center entrance hall that ran the depth of the house, with the remaining space allocated to the drawing room, the library, and the dining room. These rooms were not entirely separate, but opened off to each other through broad doorways. The plan stood in stark contrast to standard house interiors of the pre–Civil War era in America, with each distinct room separated from other rooms and halls by doors. It was the beginning of an open plan that marks the house as "modern" and American. Both the architect-supported Shingle Style and the more vernacular Queen Anne styles were based on the combination of historical detailing and open, modern room arrangements found first in the Watts Sherman House.

The house experienced three major additions, all of which were built during the lifetime of William Watts Sherman. Those responsible for these additions attempted to retain, as much as possible, the design integrity of Richardson's work. However, over the years the intended compactness of the building has been lost. The commission for the Shermans was finished in 1876, and, by 1881, an addition was necessary. This was designed by Stanford White, then a partner in his own firm. Along with this addition, White redecorated three of the main rooms. In 1890, the first of two additions designed by Dudley Newton (1845–1907), a Newport architect, was made. The resultant sprawling house is no longer completely true to Richardson and White's original vision, but the main block with its large gable organizing the façade was to profoundly influence American architecture in the 1880s and into the 1890s.

What most clearly remains of the original Watts Sherman House is the dominant gable on the façade, with a long band of windows set above a shingled pent roof. Tinted stucco is used with half-timbering inside the main gable, adding a warm coloration to the façade. Elsewhere, the upper walls are shingles over balloon framing, allowing greater construction flexibility, reflected in multiple smaller gables, bay windows, and recessed and projecting porches. Although the use of wooden shingles was one of

TOP: *Stylized fruit and floral designs such as these were popular elements in the English Arts and Crafts design movement of the 1870s, which influenced the American Queen Anne style.*

BOTTOM: *A mix of materials—wood, stone, and brick—and the incorporation of different colors and textures from the use of these materials, provided some of the visual richness that characterized the Queen Anne style*

The parlor of the Watts Sherman House was decorated in 1879–80 by Stanford White. The combined motifs from American Colonial, Oriental, and Medieval sources reflect the design freedom of the Queen Anne style.

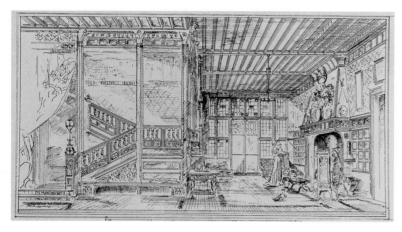

The published view of the Watts Sherman House staircase inspired thousands of imitators, and helped to transform this English-born style into an American one. Note that the sketch is a mirror image or reversed from the actual stairs. This was the inevitable consequence of the engraving and printing process used to create the illustrations of the period.

OPPOSITE: *An upstairs window seat expands to create a beautiful glass wall lighting the top of the staircase.*

Richardson's outstanding innovations, the wooden sections of the house facilitate a fussiness of detailing and articulation that is more typical of the older Gothic Revival style. The Shingle Style that emerged from the Watts Sherman House actually took its characteristic massing cues from the non-Shingled part of the house.

The main gable surmounts the extended porte cochere, allowing visitors to alight from carriages and later, automobiles, without danger of sun or rain. This feature was never part of medieval life, and neither were the small porches and balconies on the upper floors that provide views out to Narragansett Bay. Such extensions of a house into the landscape were purely American ideas of the Romantic era, and they were refined and retained in the Queen Anne house.

For all that it was a summer residence, the Watts Sherman House is still very much a proper nineteenth-century environment. No indoor-outdoor living was really imagined by the wealthy at this time. There was a terrace, but no covered porch from which to view the sea. That was a trait of tourist hotels, not genteel homes of the time. The interior decoration gives no hint of "summer house" either. The richness of materials, patterns, and decoration were embellished throughout the Sherman tenure, particularly during the decorative campaign of 1879 and 1880. The deep carved shell motif over the library fireplace recalls Newport's colonial heritage of furniture making. This is part of the decoration of the house credited specifically to Stanford White, and it certainly points to his emerging interest in the Colonial Revival style. But the sensual pleasures of the room also come from the green and gold colors used in the woodwork, and the decorative plaster work of the ceiling. Like many Queen Anne interiors, the design borrows freely motifs from around the world—American colonial, English Jacobean, even Oriental, as suggested in the gilded interlacing on the library wall.

The interior is defined by the wooden central staircase, which has solid panels built into the run of balusters, thus creating a room within a room of the stairs themselves. Revealing and concealing at the same time, the stairs create a solid center to the house with their deep mahogany paneling glowing with years of patina and polish. The cozy "look-out" created on the second floor landing by the bay window in the staircase affords a place to sit that is both within the house and projecting into the landscape. The tiny windowpanes emulate the old-fashioned windows of seventeenth-century England, but the sheer number of windows throughout the Watts Sherman House would have been astonishing to any traveler of the period. Although there is an influence of the English country house from good Queen Anne's era, the entire ensemble could only be from the latter nineteenth century.

The house has been part of Salve Regina University since 1982, and prior to that, it was used institutionally for at least six decades. Although the house has not seen the personal attention that was lavished upon it in the first decades of its existence, the richly decorated main rooms still astonish, and the exterior forms clearly proclaim their heritage of the American Queen Anne style. 🞕

ROOSEVELT HOUSE, SAGAMORE HILL, LONG ISLAND, NEW YORK

BEFORE THEODORE ROOSEVELT WAS President of the United States (1901–1908); before he served as the Governor of New York State; and even before he made the name "Roughrider" a household word during the Spanish-American War, he was a young lawyer seeking to establish a family in a home of his own. Teddy Roosevelt married the beautiful Alice Lee on his twenty-second birthday in 1880. When they returned from their honeymoon trip to Europe, an almost-standard feature of wealthy Americans' nuptials in the late Victorian era, they moved into half of a grand New York City townhouse shared with Teddy's mother, the indomitable Martha Bulloch Roosevelt. It is no surprise that the young couple began to search for their own place for a summer retreat, away from the city and its familial and social obligations.

The Roosevelts decided on a ninety-five-acre tract of forest, salt marsh, and bay beach on the northern shore of Long Island, on the Sound. Though they purchased the land in 1880, construction of a new house was not begun immediately; and then it was delayed with the death of Alice Roosevelt two days after giving birth to a daughter in 1884. His mother also died the same day, and the young man left New York and its environs altogether to mourn their loss and reconstruct his life. Roosevelt went to the Badlands of Dakota Territory, and lived the life of a cowboy, big-game hunter, and rancher for nearly two years.

He returned East in 1886 and then went to London, where he met and married Edith Carow, an American. When they returned to New York, they had a summer home all ready for them. It seems Roosevelt had kept in touch with his architect and followed through with his intention to build his house on the North Shore of Long Island, even through the years of travel and isolation. Sagamore Hill, as it became known, was created as an up-to-date residence by leading New York architects, utilizing the Shingle Style and Queen Anne style currently in vogue, and was the perfect embodiment of the American summer house.

The architectural firm Lamb and Rich was well known in the 1880s for its residential work in the tonier suburbs, its young principals being an embodiment of privilege and the Eastern establishment. Charles Rich (1854–1943) studied at Dartmouth, and upon graduation, moved to Boston and apprenticed in the office of William Ralph Emerson (1833–1917), one of the architects who developed the American Shingle Style. Rich stayed only a few years in Emerson's office, working as a general assistant and draftsman, and then left for a tour abroad in 1879–1881, considered a standard part of training for a high-society architect at the time. Rich traveled to France, Spain, Russia, and even Egypt, in search of the interesting and the exotic in architecture. As a traveling American, he may even have met the Roosevelts, in Europe during the same period; if not, they all traveled in the same circles back in New York and, as contemporaries in age would have crossed paths many times.

Charles Rich formed a partnership in New York in 1881 with Hugh Lamb, who was by all accounts the businessman of the two, while Rich did the designing. One of their first designs was a cottage in Short Hills, New Jersey, for Charles Rich's father, which in turn brought other residential commissions in that suburban enclave. Charles Rich then designed a summer house for himself in Bellport, Long Island, which is near the land Teddy Roosevelt had purchased for his own summer place. Charles Rich undertook the design of the house for Teddy Roosevelt, although it was constructed largely during Roosevelt's mourning period, when he was far away from the site.

Charles Rich would go on to become noted for architectural work at Dartmouth College as well as for country houses of grand scale. The house at Sagamore Hill is still one of his early efforts, but one done without much intervention from a client. Toward the end of his western sojourn, Roosevelt did have stuffed animal heads—trophies of his hunting adventures—sent to the house to be included in the décor of the main hall. Rich's reaction is not noted, but it seems from this and other designs that Rich was more inclined to include things rather than eliminate them from his houses. Indeed, at the very time the Roosevelt house was being designed, the prominent architectural critic Montgomery Schuyler skewered Lamb and Rich's exuberant work with such venom, it is almost comic:

> Their fragments [of houses] only recur to memory as the blurred images of a hideous dream.
> So one recalls the Batavian grace of the bulbous gables, the oriel-windows so set as to seem in
> imminent danger of toppling out, the egg and dart molding niggled up and down jambs of
> brick…the decorative details fished from the slums of the Rococo. These are not subjects for
> architectural criticism; they call for the intervention of an architectural police. …They are
> the most discreditable buildings ever erected in New York, and it is to be noted that they are
> thoroughly characteristic of the period.[33]

Schuyler's comments reflect the academic critical stance of the American architectural community toward the expressive Queen Anne style, which although not named can be imagined from the details he calls out.

Although capable of such expressive architecture, the house Rich designed for Theodore Roosevelt is, in fact, relatively simple and free of extraneous ornament. It was a summer house, and so dominated by broad porches, to provide shade and a view to Long Island Sound. That is apparently exactly what Roosevelt wanted. He wrote:

> I wished a big piazza, very broad at the n.w. corner where we could in rocking chairs look at the
> sunset; a library with a shallow bay window opening south, the parlor or drawing room occupy-
> ing all the western end of the lower floor; as broad a hall as our space would permit; big fire-
> places for logs; on the top floor the gun room occupying the western end so that north and west
> it looked over the Sound and Bay.[34]

These instructions to the architect reflect the acute sensitivity to the environment that underpinned Theodore Roosevelt's lifelong interest in nature and its conservation. On the expansive private estate he created for himself, a house could be sited with views of sunsets in mind, and no thought given to ordinary constraints like street layout.

The base of the house is a rusticated stone. The first floor is red brick, with red mortar giving a uniform, mellow appearance to the wall. The masonry base gives the house a solidity, and warm, integral color, related to English Queen Anne–style houses.

Sagamore Hill's upper floors are covered with shingles, and there is also on the house clapboard siding, panels between the banded windows. Together they give the multiplicity of textures and materials so characteristic of American Queen Anne style.

The façade is dominated by a broad gable, and it is likely that the image of the Watts Sherman House of a decade earlier was in Rich's mind. The gable defines the center of the house and its main entry is

Even as Sagamore Hill was being constructed, Roosevelt instructed the architect to make room for some hunting "trophies" he had collected in the American West.

The beamed ceiling, and the division of the wall into a lower field and upper frieze, were both typical of the Queen A

OPPOSITE: *The kitchen of Sagamore Hill is dominated by a coal stove and wo*

within this section; rambling wings extend to either side of the main block in an almost vernacular simplicity. Despite the three-and-a-half story height of the house, strong horizontal lines in the banded materials, banded windows, and controlled roof slopes keep the building in balance. Four tall brick chimneys, decorated with panels, provide the decorative pins needed to keep this rambling house from taking flight.

Queen Anne–design motifs are visible in the array of windows on the house, including bay windows, grouped windows, and an extravagant use of plate glass. Small panes, formed with wooden muntins, create decorative windows in the top sash, or in transoms above the main windows. These provided the proper "old-fashioned" look to counterbalance the modernity of the large plate glass used in the operable part of the window.

Half-timbering details on the dormers and gables, and the use of terra-cotta sunflower-motif panels on the main façade of the house are fully consistent with two common elements of the English Queen Anne style. But Sagamore Hill is

as American as its owner, for the overall effect of the house is not of decorations piled on top of each other, but of a comfortable house, which only on closer inspection reveals the richness of its ancestry and the sophistication of its apparent simplicity.

Inside, the main entry leads to a large center hall, surrounded by library, dining room, and drawing room. The Queen Anne notion of the Living Hall, the symbolic gathering space in the center of the house, is expressed here in a kind of shorthand with a widening of a traditional center hall and the insertion of a decorative fireplace. In fact, the plan of Sagamore Hill has less in common with the open plans promoted in many high-style houses of the period, like the Watts Sherman House, and more in common with the formality of pre–Civil War houses. Each room has distinct and rather narrow door openings to the hall. The main rooms do not interconnect with each other, although the drawing room does have direct access to the porch.

Certainly, the grand staircase with its paneling up the walls is impressive and vaguely medieval, as the Queen Anne style was conceived of originally, but it is also very practical in a summer house that was intended to contain the vigorous life of a large and boisterous family. Theodore and Edith had five children, four of them boys, and they all were encouraged by their father to be active, play outdoors, and not take conventional manners too seriously.

The house contains twenty-three rooms on three floors, including a large room added by the Roosevelts in 1905, during Theodore's U.S. presidency, to receive officials and to display the many trophies, books, paintings, and artifacts given to him. Its eclectic architecture, with classical columns and a medieval

A projecting gable forms a porte cochere, where carriages could drop off a guest to the front door without exposing them to sun or rain.

vaulted ceiling and massive fireplace, was still within the aesthetic of the Queen Anne style, though constructed a generation after the initial appearance of the style in the United States.

Sagamore Hill was home to the Roosevelt family until 1950, and then passed to the Theodore Roosevelt Association, a nonprofit corporation founded upon Theodore Roosevelt's death to memorialize him and his achievements. The Association granted the house and eighty-three remaining acres of the property to the U.S. National Park Service in 1963, who have maintained it ever since. Thus, Sagamore Hill uniquely contains its original family's furnishings and memorabilia. Sagamore Hill is a monument to the talents and achievements of an extraordinary man, Theodore Roosevelt. In his choice of style for his home, by a man who could have built anything, he reflected the emerging popular taste for the Queen Anne in domestic architecture that was to dominate America from 1880 to 1900. 🍥

The front entrance includes a "Dutch" door, with the upper part able to be opened to let in light and air while the lower part stayed closed to secure children and pets.

EDWARD BROOKE HOUSE, BIRDSBORO, PENNSYLVANIA

FRANK FURNESS (1839–1912) is often cited as an architect whose output was uniquely distinctive, arising from his own particular genius. He grew up in the Romanticism of antebellum America, and took to heart the advice of the era's philosopher, Ralph Waldo Emerson, who wrote in one essay, "Whoso would be a man, must be a nonconformist. …I hope in these days we have heard the last of conformity and consistency."[35]

Furness was an adventurer seeking to create an "American" style out of forms inherited from Europe, and he could not have been less of a conformist to earlier classical styles and to the delicate, "pretty" Romantic work of the 1850s. Furness's work may be best characterized as masculine. He began his practice in Philadelphia after the Civil War, and his architecture gave expression to the yearning to create bold new forms for a new age dominated by invention and machine technology.

Furness is perhaps best known for the Pennsylvania Academy of Fine Arts Building (1872–1876) in Philadelphia, his home city. The Pennsylvania Academy of Fine Arts uses a modern plan and technical innovations in materials, but presents them in a modified Gothic Revival style, where decoration is rich and prolific. Decoration in architecture, as in furnishings and decorative arts, expressed the material prosperity of the United States after the Civil War; the richness of color, pattern, and materials that we associate with the Victorian era is really the exuberant manifestation of material wealth, a wealth that was unknown in this country up to that time. Furness's decorative, colorful buildings drew attention to themselves and to their clever architect. Attention brought commissions, and in the decade following the construction of the Pennsylvania Academy of Fine Arts, he became one of the most popular and successful architects in Philadelphia.

Furness was well acquainted with the social and business elite of Philadelphia in the 1870s and 80s. Furness had grown up there, the son of a prominent Unitarian minister, and thus enjoyed a comprehensive liberal education and family connections to some of the most progressive people in the city. Frank Furness served in the Civil War, in a cavalry unit, from 1861 to 1865, and on his return to civilian life, was recognized as a decorated war hero, with a bearing and attitude that commanded attention and respect.

From 1858 to 1861 Furness trained in the New York atelier of Richard Morris Hunt, the pre-eminent architect in the United States from 1850 to 1880. Furness had a talent for design and drawing, but did not study abroad, or attend the Massachusets Institute of Technology, which in 1866 instituted the first academic degree program in architecture in the United States. Frank Furness learned his craft in apprenticeships and on-the-job training, qualities that made him "one of the boys" with so many of the self-made industrialists and merchants who shaped America in the years after the Civil War.

Little wonder that Furness—for all his stylistic originality—was granted the license to be creative and individualistic by his peers, who flooded him with commissions. From 1867 to 1889, he designed over three hundred buildings. Civic buildings, banks, railroad stations, and residences were all part of the output of his firm, first Furness & Hewitt (1871–1875) and later, Furness & Evans. The Furness firm, while working to achieve a decided originality in many commissions, was also not unconnected to the larger fashions of architectural taste. Thus it was in the 1880s that Furness relied upon many elements of the Queen Anne style to create the Edward Brooke House in Birdsboro, Pennsylvania.

Edward Brooke (1863–1933) was the third generation of a family closely associated with the development of the iron industry in the Schuylkill River Valley. His father and uncle had transformed a small,

local ironworks into a major producer of iron. Under Edward, Sr., and his brother George's stewardship, the Birdsboro Furnace took advantage of a unique location to utilize local iron ore as the raw material, fired the furnaces with the region's newly available anthracite coal, and loaded the iron ore into barges onto Hay Creek, which ran through town. From there, the iron was easily transported to industrial communities downriver, like Phoenixville, Pottstown, and of course, Philadelphia. The Birdsboro Furnace employed hundreds of men, making the small community of Birdsboro (incorporated 1872) a "company town" whose fortunes would rise in the latter nineteenth century with the prosperity of the local iron works, and decline with it at the close of World War II.

Edward Brooke, Jr. married in 1887, and his family commissioned Frank Furness to design a grand house on a hill as a gift to Edward and Louise Clingan, his bride. Completed in 1888, the house was sited on a hill overlooking the Schuylkill River Valley, and the iron works that brought Brooke the resources with which to build his palatial country house. The Brookes lived in Philadelphia, on fashionable Rittenhouse Square, but used the Birdsboro house as a country retreat, and to maintain a family presence in their company town.

The "Brooke Mansion" as it was appropriately called, contained forty-two rooms on three floors, plus a full basement. Because it was not to be used full-time the walls were lined with sheets of iron, in the belief that it would make the house fireproof. Shutters were built in to every window so that when the house was closed up, sunlight would not damage the furnishings within, and keep prying eyes out. The house showcases ironwork as a decorative feature, alluding to the material that built the Brooke family fortune.

The Edward Brooke House also incorporated a variety of exotic woods in its interior finishes, including quarter-sawn oak, African mahogany, rosewood, and ebony. Fireplaces incorporated tile, limestone, granite, and brick. The lavish interior, focused on the two-story entry and stair-hall, and complete with over a dozen bedrooms, was the perfect setting for the young couple to entertain family and friends for extended stays.

While highly original, and a testament to Frank Furness's design talent, the Brooke House has all the elements of the Queen Anne style, although undoubtedly at a grander scale than most. Furness had declared his interest in "naturalism," by which he meant a freedom of plan and elevation proceeding from the inside out in regard to the layout of rooms and the subsequent placement of windows and doors, and this showed in the free plan of the Brooke House. The asymmetry of the Queen Anne in its best aspects is just this—not a willful disregard of the classical canons of symmetry but the expression of an emerging freedom, modernism if you will, in architecture. Furness's "naturalism" was easiest to explore in large country houses like the Brookes', as there were no constraints of nearby buildings to block light, or views to be avoided.

The house is built into its hillside with a heavy rusticated stone base and first floor, while the upper floors are shingled in mahogany (for durability, and nearly all the originals are intact and in place). A tower anchors the corner of the main portion of the house, and the service wing trails out behind it, but all rooms, particularly on the upper floors, whether for master or servant, command a view of the rolling countryside.

At the first-floor level, a porch wraps around the tower, the heavy stone forming the porch balustrade, and providing a sense of seclusion and shelter, even as the low arches frame vistas of open space. From the porch, there are two entries into the house—one through the formal vestibule, decorated with an elaborate metalwork screen, and the other from the porte cochere. Both lead into the high L-shaped hall,

The round library, in the base of the tower, includes a fireplace whose tiled facing and built-in mirror above also reflect the circular plan of the room.

The vast living hall of the Edward Brooke House includes the staircase seen in a previous photo, this fireplace of rusticated stone, and ample space for seating, while it retains its role as the central hall, with other major rooms leading off of it.

lighted with stained and leaded glass from both ends of the space. Typical of the Queen Anne style, the hallway is dominated by the staircase, rising to a landing that forms a sort of high stage. Theatrical entrances by Mrs. Brooke, who could survey arriving guests from the landing window and then sweep down the stairs to greet them, were practically guaranteed. The heavy newel post has a large classical swag carved into it, a decorative design that is found in other works of the period by Furness. This reminds us that at its heart, Queen Anne started as a revival of classical design, although it acquired many other design heritages in its evolution in the United States in the 1880s. The staircase landing is relieved of strict classicism however by incorporating a wooden carving of a cherub holding a lightbulb. Decoration and technology were interwoven in all Queen Anne houses to some extent, and to a very high degree in this house.

The hall itself contains a fireplace of massive boulders, the interior manifestation of the exterior's rocky foundation and base. Carved wood brackets and overmantle in the stone fireplace connect it to the wood beams and wainscot in the room.

Off the hall, in the base of the tower is the remarkable round library. The built-in rosewood shelves are fitted to the round walls, as is the fireplace on one side of the room. Built-in seats under the windows provide a perfect place to curl up and read, under the large, slightly curved panes of glass that complete the circumference of the room.

Across the hall from the library, a wide opening leads to Mr. Brooke's study. The room can be closed off for privacy with gliding pocket doors of paneled oak, their beautiful smooth finish still original from 1888. The library also has a fireplace, with a massive oak mantle. French doors lead from this room directly outside to the porch, perhaps to allow Mr. Brooke and his visitors to have a cigar. A safe built into the back of the room provided for the financial security of the family and their business.

The so-called "Ladies Parlor," with views across the valley, ranged along the center of the house. In this large and airy room, rare African mahogany woodwork is lighter in tone than in the dark library, and less aggressively grained than that found in the more masculine office. The original electric light fixture survives in this room, a complex multiarmed affair that would have dazzled evening visitors used to candlelight or gaslight. The fireplace in the Ladies Parlor has an unusual stone mantel and wooden overmantel. The sinuous design anticipates in some ways European Art Nouveau design, but it is pure Frank Furness.

A final passage leads off the main entrance hall, lined with beautifully paneled closets for receiving guests' cloaks; a special closet retains the wooden knobs that would allow a custom-made riding whip to rest without tangling or being bent. This short hall leads into a dining room, which is also accessible from the Ladies Parlor. Dominated by a hip-roofed, hooded fireplace, a rather medieval-looking design favored by Richard Norman Shaw, the English architect whose designs launched the Queen Anne style, the dining room is a warm, comfortable space. However, Shaw never used a mantel like this, it was created at the Brooke family foundries of cast iron, another testament to the material that built the entire house. The cast iron would have heated up and radiated quite nicely on a chill morning. The relatively modest size of the room and the functional fireplace suggest that the Brookes used this as a family dining room, and if they entertained many guests formally for dinner, may have done so in the center hall.

Behind the dining room, a vast service wing, nearly equal in size to the formal, front part of the house, provided the support for its operation. Butleries, kitchen, pantries, laundry, and servants' rooms were busy whenever the Brookes' were in residence. According to U.S. Census records, the Brookes typically had five live-in servants in the period 1890–1900: a cook, a housemaid, a chambermaid, and two gardeners. As automobiles became available, the Brooke family purchased one, and then hired a chauffeur to drive it. He lived in an apartment over the garage/stable (now a separate property). Local lore places the number of servants at nineteen, which may have been true when including locals who worked in the house but did not live there, or including those hired for special occasions.

Although there were plenty of servants to help run the household, the house itself was also built with modern technology in mind. The Queen Anne style embraced technology in the same way it embraced decorative elements. The Brookes' house had a massive coal-fired furnace in the basement, leading steam to radiators in the primary rooms that were often cleverly concealed in built-in window seats to minimize their visual intrusion. The house had a built-in vacuum system installed in 1888, a system that still works. Although far out in the country, the Birdsboro Furnace and Steel Company had its own electric dynamo from an early date, and it was through this company power plant that the Brooke house was supplied. Electricity was clearly the power source for the future, but pressurized gas was widely known and available. Thus, the house includes fixtures for both electricity and gas; a not uncommon situation for American houses of the 1880s and 90s. Also reflecting its originally somewhat isolated, country location, the house was fitted with a security system, which worked by scaring intruders with the sound of bells, but could not have summoned help from off-site.

The Brookes' maintained separate bedrooms on the second floor, as was the custom among the upper classes in the Victorian era. Mrs. Brooke's room is at the second-floor level of the tower. The woodwork is again light in tone, and the room's focus is the blue tile fireplace. An adjoining sitting room has a unique half-round window, fitted with removable shutters.

Mr. Brooke's bedroom, across the broad landing, has a more conventional fireplace, with tiles using the sunflower motif—one of the most popular decorative motifs of the latter nineteenth century. The room has a gas jet on a folding arm projecting from the wall, at a height mid-way up the wall. Was this intended to provide over-the-shoulder light to someone who loved to read in bed? Or allow for a heat source for one to stand and warm a before-bedtime drink? The exact use is unknown, but the presence of another "gadget" in Mr. Brooke's room affirms his love of technology. Both Mr. and Mrs. Brookes' rooms are fitted "en suite," with a tiled bathroom, and the latest porcelain fixtures of the day.

The third floor includes a nursery in the turret, where, again, built-in cabinetry emphasizes the roundness of the room. It is banded with light, as windows encircle the room, and it offers a scenic vista to wooded hills. Daydreaming in this tower room, one could easily imagine soaring with the hawks that hang over the distant hills, rising with the thermals coming up from the valley.

Down the long halls of the third floor, servants' rooms, now empty, recall their function through their plain, undecorated plaster walls and utilitarian linoleum flooring. However, the survival of original linoleum here offers a glimpse of yet another new material of the Queen Anne period, selected for its easy-to-clean, "sanitary" qualities and its bright coloring. The Brookes' servants were treated to quarters far better than many householders lived in—no dirty, discolored old carpet for them! The elaborate call box mounted in one room reminds us that the servants were always "on call," even when they retired to their rooms for well-deserved rest at the end of the day.

The Edward Brooke House remains in private ownership, although no longer in possession of the Brooke family. Without two full-time gardeners on staff, the landscaped surroundings of the house have become much simpler than they would have been. The considerable property that once accompanied the Brooke House has been sold off over the years to create a pleasant residential neighborhood, but the newer houses are almost toylike in comparison to the large scale and robust materials of the mansion itself. Some of the mill buildings, railroad sidings, and sheds remain in the village of Birdsboro, testifying to the industrial legacy of the community, while the Edward Brooke House remains high above, a "queen" among commoners, and the magnificent consort of the memory of Frank Furness. ✸

The main doorway incorporates elaborate glasswork, and artistic metalwork. Metals were the basis of the Brooke family's fortune, so it was fitting that Furness showcased the material throughout the house.

CASTLE HILL, NEWPORT, RHODE ISLAND

"CASTLE HILL" WAS ALREADY A LANDMARK for sailors in Narragansett Bay in the eighteenth century, although there was no castle on it, and the hill was only forty feet above sea level. But the name has clung to the forty-acre peninsula of land at the southwestern end of the city of Newport for all these years. The Narragansett Bay provided a sheltering harbor for ships in the eighteenth century, making Newport one of the wealthiest of colonial America's port cities. But as ships got bigger, the rocky inlets were no longer so welcoming, and Newport's economic importance dwindled; instead of a bustling merchant center it became a quiet town of old colonial houses. The beautiful setting however remained attractive to those who loved the ocean, and in the latter nineteenth century, Newport once again rose to prominence, this time, as a summer resort destination.

Newport was just coming into its own as a summer resort in the 1870s. On the eastern side of the city, a wealthy young couple from Boston, Mr. and Mrs. William Watts Sherman, had just commissioned a summer house from H. H. Richardson. The peninsula called Castle Hill was purchased in 1874 by Alexander Agassiz (1835–1910), and his sister Pauline and her husband, Quincy Shaw, of Boston. Quincy Shaw was a Boston Brahmin of the highest rank and fortune; the Agassiz family loved the sea. Alexander Agassiz was recently widowed, but had three sons. So it seemed perfectly right for the families to purchase land in Newport, and to look forward to spending their summers there on the breezy hill with views to the water of the Narragansett Bay. Two houses were built in 1875 for the two families on the peninsula; Agassiz to the north side, and the Shaws to the south.

Agassiz was a scientist, with interests in zoology, oceanography, and marine science, which he learned at Harvard and at his father's knee. The only son of Louis Agassiz (1807–1873), perhaps the most famous scientist of the mid-nineteenth century, Alexander shared his father's interest in fish and geology, but he did not follow his father into the theological and scientific debates that led Agassiz senior to spend much of the latter part of his life arguing against Darwin's theory of evolution. As a young man, Alexander Agassiz took his knowledge of science, in particular of geology, to mining companies, and he became spectacularly rich through his investments in American copper mines in the Upper Midwest. With a fortune secured, he returned to Harvard, and to academic life, in 1870. He became curator of the museum at the Lawrence Scientific School at Harvard, which was begun with his father's collections. He taught and traveled to collect specimens of animals and minerals from around the world, and continued to strengthen the study of science in America through his support of the National Academy of Sciences, the American Association for the Advancement of Science, and numerous other scientific societies and organizations.

But his first love was the marine life of the Atlantic Ocean, and so it is not surprising that he chose to create a summer retreat where he could be near the ocean and its creatures. In order to instill this love in his students, he installed a laboratory in his house, and invited students to come visit him in the summer to study marine life there. Professor Agassiz developed and helped to fund Harvard's marine laboratory and student research center at Castle Hill until 1898, when the researchers and their efforts outgrew his house. The work carried on, however, and developed into the Woods Hole Oceanographic Institute, one of the most prestigious centers for the study of marine biology in the world today.

As a measure of the importance of Newport as a summer gathering for the rich, the famous, and the important of the day, the *New York Times* through the 1880s and 90s carried notes from Newport in its social columns. Alexander Agassiz appears, occasionally, in these notes. For instance, in 1882, it noted that

An elaborate Moorish-inspired overmantel design dominates the living hall of Castle Hill,
which includes the broad, open stairs in one corner of the room.

A graceful bell-cast top to the tower gives Castle Hill a distinctive profile.

he was entertaining the Town and Country Club, which was, in fact, the literary and scientific association of Newport, limited to fifty members. Another "Notes from Newport" column in 1898 presented a long list of luncheons, dinners, dances, receptions, and horse shows; in the midst of these social activities was the rather earnest announcement that "Professor Alexander Agassiz will entertain the Town and Country Club...at the Casino Theater next Friday afternoon, when he will read a paper on 'The Fiji Islands and Coral Reefs.'"[36]

Agassiz's home-laboratory work and eager students made his summer cottage feel rather cramped. In 1880, his sister and brother-in-law sold him their house; soon thereafter, that cottage burned down. With the whole peninsula for himself and his work, Agassiz planned to build a larger house that could accommodate his research, his students, and his sons and their friends.

Typical of the professor's low-key style, he did not hire Richard Morris Hunt, a fellow member of the Town and Country Club and perhaps the leading architect of America at the time. Besides, Hunt was busy building the lavish palaces up on Bellevue Avenue for the Vanderbilts, creating an American Imperial style of architecture from bits of neoclassicism and lots of marble. In fact, Agassiz did not even hire an architect. Instead, he turned to Thomas and George Shaw, brothers who were experienced builders, to transform the old cottage on his property into a large, new house.

The wealthiest Americans who came to Newport commissioned their own summer "cottages" and although perhaps the first of these from the 1860s, may have had some relationship to the term, by the Gilded Age, the term "Newport cottage" was used as a tongue-in-cheek allusion to a palatial villa. The most desirable building lots had access to the broad avenues, so that those taking carriage drives could see and be seen; and also access to water views and to sea breezes. Perhaps any other Newport denizen who owned a peninsula already named "Castle Hill" would have found it irresistible to build the castle that could be seen for miles upon the water.

But Alexander Agassiz had no interest in flaunting his fortune or his residence. The house that he had built in 1883 is a fine example of American Queen Anne architecture. It is clad completely in shingles, leading to some attributions as a Shingle Style dwelling, but the vernacular nature of its design and construction makes it part of the Queen Anne tradition. A portion of the original cottage, which was described as "Swiss style" by contemporaries in the 1870s, is still visible in the central block of the house, where the front entry is located. The third-floor dormer and gable, with their board-and-batten siding and hipped roof with deep eaves on brackets, are visually related to other Swiss or Stick Style houses of the 1870s.[37] But these are only fragmentary survivors in a house that today is dominated by a four-story, hexagonal tower under a bell-cast roof, and a broad sweep of porch. The house lacks applied ornament, gaining interest from the texture of the shingled walls, and the different geometric shapes—cylinder, rectangle, triangle—that are clearly playing off each other. The windows are large, but simple—no complex muntin patterns here as in many Queen Anne–

The layering of wooden shingle siding, vertical siding, clapboards, and wooden trim gives this wooden structure complexity and richness of detail.

style houses. It is as if the sharp breezes from the Bay scoured off any extra fussiness, leaving behind the solid, comfortable house that would endure cold winters and be ready to welcome its occupants back when the summer came again.

Castle Hill is a huge wooden house, and the extensions of porte cochere, sunroom, porches, and service wings in all directions from the main block of the house create the asymmetrical, rambling form that perfectly defined the Queen Anne style. From the lowest-level service areas to the lookout room in the top of the tower, the house contains five floors of living space.

Alexander Agassiz died in 1910, on board a ship returning him to the United States after travel to Europe. His will, probated in Newport, divided his considerable fortune among his sons, his servants, and the institutions that he had supported all his adult life. He left $200,000 to Harvard University and $50,000 each to the American Academy of Arts and Sciences, and the National Academy of Science.[38] His family retained the Newport house until 1939, when they sold it to J. T. O'Connell. The large rambling house has served as a hotel ever since. In 2003, The Inn at Castle Hill, as it is now known, was completely and carefully restored. 🍂

CHARLES BALDWIN HOUSE, NEWPORT, RHODE ISLAND

CHARLES H. BALDWIN'S LIFE (1822–1888) forms the material of an exciting adventure story. Born in New York City just as it was emerging as the leading city of the United States, he joined the navy in 1839 and saw action in the Mexican–American War. He commanded the steamer *Clifton* in the Civil War, working the Gulf Coast and then heading up the Mississippi to participate in the first attack on Vicksburg in 1862. Following the Civil War, he and his young family moved to California, where he served on Mare Island. Baldwin served well in each post, and was regularly promoted up through the ranks. He and his wife had a busy social life at their home on Fifth Avenue in New York City, and when they traveled together. The society pages noted that the couple attended the 1878 Exposition Universelle, the third international exposition of arts and industry held in Paris, celebrating the recovery of France after the crushing defeat of the 1870 Franco–Prussian War. He was named a commodore in 1876, and was sent by the United States government as its official representative to the coronation of Tsar Alexander III of Russia in 1881. In 1883, he became a rear-admiral, one of the highest ranks available in the navy during peacetime, and was assigned to command the Mediterranean squadron.

As a balance to this peripatetic life, Commodore Baldwin built a summer house in Newport, Rhode Island, near to the sea he loved, in 1878. He named the house "Snug Harbor," a sly reference to the home for retired sailors maintained by the U.S. Navy on Staten Island, as Baldwin was on the verge of retirement from active sea duty when he built it. But Baldwin's Newport home was considerably grander than the name "Snug Harbor" might suggest, and it is not, in fact, on the water, but right in the middle of the most fashionable stretch of Bellevue Avenue, in the most fashionable summer resort of the latter nineteenth century.

Baldwin's house was designed by Potter and Robertson, an architectural firm practicing in New York. In 1877, when it was designed, the Queen Anne style was still new, and somewhat local, with its first American-built example, the Watts Sherman House, standing only a few blocks away. Of the architectural partners, William C. Potter (1842–1909) was the better known at the time, having designed with his brother, Edward, a series of churches and collegiate buildings—most notably for Union College and Princeton University. William Potter's interest in ecclesiastical buildings led him to a great familiarity with the Gothic Revival and Romanesque Revival styles, and he used these forms for post offices and customs houses in the 1870s when he served as the Supervising Architect of the United States Government. It is perhaps through government connections that Potter and Commodore Baldwin met.

The Baldwin House is a rare example of domestic architecture attributed to William Potter, and it builds on his strong knowledge of Gothic and Medieval architecture. Potter's architectural partner during the years 1875–1878 was Robert Robertson (1849–1919), who had learned architecture under New York architect George B. Post. Like Post, Robertson's best-known buildings are commercial ones, and both worked on projects that helped to define the modern American skyscraper. The combination of Potter's historicism and Robertson's functional bent brought forth "Snug Harbor," a fully realized Queen Anne–style mansion that incorporated all the right medieval details of half-timbered gabled and paneled brick chimneys and irregular gables and rooflines, with an open plan, and a modern interior conception of space and room layout. Potter and Robertson were clearly proud of the house they planned for Commodore Baldwin, for it was published in *The American Architect and Building News* in March of 1878, some three months before construction was even complete.

Guests to the summer house of Commodore and Mrs. Charles H. Baldwin arrived under the shelter of the projecting porte cochere.

The large and geometrically complex house built for *Commodore Charles Baldwin in 1878 was published that same year in* The American Architect and Building News. *Queen Anne architecture was presented and popularized across the nation through magazines and other serial publications, more than any popular architectural style before it.*

A long and detailed article—perhaps written by the architects—was also published at the same time, and the text gives a clear idea of the features that made the Baldwin house remarkable in its day. This written description is also valuable today, for it shows how well preserved the house is, as nearly all features mentioned in the 1878 article are still extant:

A very tasty appearing villa, after plans by Messrs. Potter and Robertson of New York, will be completed in early June for Commodore C. H. Baldwin, United States Navy, of New York. It is located on Bellevue Avenue, a little south of the Ocean House, and adjoins the summer residence of the late Henry DeRahm…The house is built of brick and wood. It is 95 feet long by 65 feet wide, but owing to its being cut up it does not look as large. All the ridges in the roofs are surmounted by a combing of an antique pattern, with turned finials of wood, surmounted with iron vanes of a very neat design. The outside of the house is part shingled, clapboarded, sheathed and carved, not two of its moldings being alike, and when it is taken into consideration that there are 150 patterns, an idea can be had of the work necessary to carry out the plans.

Above the large window are smaller ones in diamond pattern, thus showing the ancient as well as modern style. A porte cochere extends over the front entrance some thirty feet, and it is of a very ancient style. The piazza piers are built of brick, two feet over the floors, and upon which rest a group of four columns, which will support its roof. The estate, when completed, will be enclosed with a brick wall which will be laid on a stone foundation six feet in depth and three feet in width. The main entrance is on the west side, facing Bellevue Avenue, and the main hall is reached through a vestibule 10 by 12 feet, which has a tile floor. An archway leads into the main hall, the steps being of marble. Turning to the left is the staircase hall where you see a window which occupies the whole…with a row of colored lights at the top.

The staircase is made of oak and black walnut, with a heavy rail of the same material. Ascending the stairs and looking to the right a row of black walnut turned columns can be seen with a fancy balustrade running around all four sides and from here an excellent view can be had of the hall. Nothing obstructs the view from the hall floor to the apex of the roof, 49 feet [above].

Window seats under large windows were popularized in American architecture in the nineteenth century.

In front of the main hall is the dining room, which is reached through an opening 8 feet wide, no doors being used. The dimensions of this room are 22 by 34 feet, and it has a fancy hardwood floor and ceiling, elegantly carved mantel and chimney breast of terra-cotta tile work. It is lighted by three large windows and there is a row of arches resting on turned columns of black walnut running the entire length of the room.[39]

That last detail—the black walnut arcade—no longer exists in the house. There are other details throughout the lengthy article, which continues for several more paragraphs, that are no longer at the house, but in general, it shows that many of the remarkable features of 1878 survive.

In the parlor, the dark wood of the beamed ceiling and the intricate parquet floor combine to give this Queen Anne interior a feeling of coziness and warmth.

A review of the details that the anonymous writer pointed out help to clarify what was new about the Queen Anne style in 1878 for an American audience. First, the multiple mentions of "antique" and "ancient" on a new house point to the purposeful creation of a building that looked backward for its design inspiration. In an era that had praised progress and "the new" more than anything else, this marked a real shift in taste.

The enumeration of the different materials and textures of the house—brick, shingle, clapboard, wood sheathing, and carving, and those 150 different moldings—points to the profusion of surfaces that would characterize even the simplest version of the American Queen Anne style over the next quarter century. Such lavish detail also begins to suggest why the house was reported to cost about $50,000, a huge sum of money for its day.

The comment about the window combining ancient and modern style with tiny diamond panes set in the transom above the large plate-glass windows also points to a feature of the Queen Anne style that would become nearly ubiquitous. There are other references, not quoted, to "colored lights," meaning panes of stained or colored glass used in places throughout the house. Much of that original colored glass did not survive in the Baldwin House, but its presence originally is absolutely typical of another favorite device of the Queen Anne house.

The openness of the interior plan is remarked upon in the note that there is no door at the opening to the dining room from the hall. A free-flowing floor plan without doors between rooms is the modern ideal, and here it is in its incipient form, called out for the reader. The openness from the hall floor up into the peak of the house is also a novel spatial move, one that was less commonly repeated in houses that needed to be occupied (and heated) during the winter.

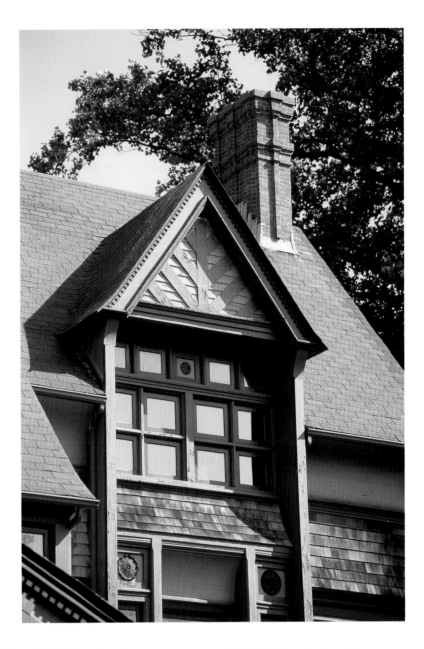

Half-timbering in the gables, even though applied as a strictly decorative element and not reflective of construction forms used in the house, was popularly used on Queen Anne–style houses.

The article names several other rooms besides the vestibule, stair hall, and dining room. These include the butler's pantry, the laundry and a drying room, two pantries, and a wine cellar, proving that a house of this size needed considerable staff and support space to operate smoothly. Upstairs on the second floor were "seven guest chambers," suggesting that the primary function of the summer house was for entertaining friends and relations.

The 1878 article notes that the guest rooms were "finished with the best of white pine and painted in five different colors." These polychromatic interior finishes are long gone, but the fact that it was remarked upon leads one to believe that "five different colors" was extraordinary by the standards of the day.

The Queen Anne–style's interest in intricate patterns extended to details like this tile vestibule floor at the Baldwin House.

Commodore Charles Baldwin and his family and friends enjoyed the house for less than a decade, before he sold the house and its furnishings in one lot for $80,000 to one Francis Carley. Charles Baldwin died in 1888; his wife, Mary, who was twenty years younger, continued to live in a cottage on the grounds of the big house for several years. Following World War I, Newport lost some of its cachet as a resort, and with the Depression, many of the grand houses in town were demolished or subdivided. The Baldwin House was converted into three apartments for some time, but with the revival of interest in the community's rich architectural legacy in the 1960s, a buyer stepped forward who was willing to convert the house back into a single-family dwelling.

The house remains a private family home, maintained as one of the outstanding, early examples of the Queen Anne style. It is clear from the publication of the Baldwin House's image and description that Potter and Robertson's design influenced a generation of American housebuilders in their acceptance of the Queen Anne style. 🌸

The rear garden view shows the variety of window sizes, types, and placement that gives each Queen Anne–style house its individuality.

Bedford Park was a development near London, England, created with houses designed by Queen Anne–style originator Richard Norman Shaw. This illustration of 1882 helped to popularize both the style and the idea of the planned suburb.

SUBURBAN HOUSES

THE ERA OF THE Queen Anne house was also the era of the suburb. New communities were laid out beyond the old borders of cities and towns, taking advantage of new, cheaper mass transportation, like railroads and streetcars. The city had long been perceived as too crowded, unsanitary, and dangerous—but it was not until the latter half of the nineteenth century that so many people could act on those perceptions and move to a greener, cleaner suburb while still maintaining economic, cultural, and social ties to the city.

Suburbs are by definition the by-products of cities; so it is not surprising that New Jersey, set between two of the largest, oldest, and most powerful cities of the United States in the nineteenth century, Philadelphia and New York, should provide the setting for several suburbs. Two of the houses discussed in the following section are in the planned community of Montrose Park, now part of the municipality of South Orange. Created as a suburb of Newark, New Jersey, and then becoming a suburb of New York as transportation in the region improved, Montrose Park tried to set high standards for building and development. The individually designed houses in the community include several Queen Anne–style examples. Not far away, a much simpler builder's development in the town of Madison also incorporated Queen Anne–style architecture, available through the published designs of a team of architects aiming to provide a touch of high style at low cost.

The community of Oak Park, Illinois, was laid out as a haven for Chicago commuters and their families in the 1890s and has thrived in that role ever since. Among the early residents were the Hemingways, whose son Ernest grew up to be a great American writer, and winner of a Nobel Prize in Literature. His childhood home, now a museum, is an excellent example of the Queen Anne style, and is very typical of its time and place. Also in Oak Park is the home of the Robert Parkers. Their house is far less typical in design, for it is one of the earliest-known works of the architect Frank Lloyd Wright. Wright would quickly leave behind the Queen Anne–style architecture he had been taught to draw and go on to create a unique vision of American architecture, the seeds of which are visible in the Parker's house.

Back on the East Coast, the Conover House in Greenwich, Connecticut, was one of the first houses erected in an emerging neighborhood outside the center of a town that was growing to be a suburb of New York. The Conover House was published, and seen by a national audience, at the height of the Queen Anne–style's popularity. The images may have solidified the taste for the early Queen Anne throughout America; but the style-conscious owners of this particular house were ready to update it by the early twentieth century. Today the Conover House displays a fascinating overlay of the evolution of the Queen Anne style, with the expressions of the later aspect of the style grafted onto one of the early published versions.

MONTROSE PARK, SOUTH ORANGE, NEW JERSEY

INDUSTRIALIZATION IN AMERICA CREATED wealth from harnessing the raw power of coal, steam, iron, and steel. The increase in heavy manufacturing also made the cities where industry concentrated dirty and smoggy. So in post-Civil War America, there was an increasing desire on the part of those who could afford it to leave the city, and establish homes in the areas around the cities. Suburbs of cities have existed since Roman times, but it is fair to say that late nineteenth-century America accelerated and popularized the phenomenon to such an extent that by the twentieth century the overwhelming ideal of an American home was a suburban one.

The Queen Anne style was a durable component of many, many suburbs. Its irregular forms were best expressed where there was some open land on all sides of the building. The variety of decorative forms used on the Queen Anne house, particularly the porches, were inevitably complemented by their extension into a landscaped setting. However modest the yard, a composition of lawn accented by some flowers or shrubs provided another opportunity for the homeowner to demonstrate an "artistic" sensibility.

No state was, or is, more suburbanized than New Jersey, and so it is no surprise that in its many communities, suburban living was defined and popularized. Noted since colonial times as "a barrel tapped at both ends" by its location between the two great cities of New York and Philadelphia, New Jersey has been the location of several landmarks of suburbanization. In the 1850s, the first planned suburb, Llewellyn Park, in West Orange, was laid out and the first houses were constructed to designs by noted architect A. J. Davis. It was not the houses themselves that distinguished Llewellyn Park, however, so much as its landscape design, which included curvilinear roads that purposely eschewed the American gridded street plan, which by the mid-nineteenth century had already spread from the streets of Manhattan to the settlement squares of the West. In addition, the attention paid to the landscape resulted in the creation of public spaces within the Llewellyn Park subdivision which took advantage of marginal developable land on the hilly, wooded site to create memorable (and marketable) retreats. Within this suburban enclave Davis created carriage drives, and a "ramble," or pathway along the craggy edge of a stream, both concepts that would be used in another decade in the design for Central Park, in New York City. Clever use of the lands less desirable for building, coupled with Romantic imagery, made the unusable into an asset for the community, a device that lingers in subdivision planning to this day.

With Llewellyn Park as an example, other suburbs were soon privately developed in New Jersey through the latter nineteenth century, although none reached the integration of landscape, urban design, and architecture achieved at Llewellyn Park. The development of Romantic suburbs coincided with the increasing desire of the wealthy and middle-class residents to leave the industrial cities. As early as 1860, another suburb was planned only a few miles from Llewellyn Park, this one called "Montrose Park." The developer of Montrose Park, New York attorney John Gorham Vose, bought a tract of former farmland, subdivided it to create curvilinear streets leading to lots of about one acre in size (compared to the ten-acre lots of Llewellyn Park, or the standard 25 x 100 foot lots of urban development), and proceeded to market the area heavily to New York and Newark's upper-middle class as a fine location for home building. Montrose Park was near both a railroad connection to those cities, and horse-drawn trolleys into Newark. The commute was expensive, though, automatically making Montrose Park available only to the wealthy.

The Civil War slowed the initial development of Montrose Park, and by 1870, Vose decided he had to build some houses speculatively to "jump start" sales, before others would be persuaded to buy empty lots and build their own houses in his planned suburb.

But not just any houses were built, for in addition to the large lot sizes, Vose kept his subdivision exclusive through the writing of restrictive covenants into each deed. In the days before zoning and other public land-use restrictions, covenants were the only way to control how a property was used, and they were usually written to create and control residential enclaves for the wealthy. In the original Montrose Park deeds of sale, the covenants limit each property to one house and outbuildings, "appropriate for a gentleman's country residence."

No industry, no commercial buildings, or even public buildings were to be allowed in Montrose Park, except for houses of worship. A single house of worship exists today within the bounds of Montrose Park, although it was not built until the mid-twentieth century. The residents' interests lay elsewhere. As early as 1880, the Orange Lawn Tennis Club was founded on ten acres within the park, located on the grounds of founder John Vose's own home after his decease in 1874. The Tennis Club was a locus of social activity; its grass courts played host to the National Tennis Championship of 1886. The club's popularity demanded that it move to larger quarters in 1916, outside of Montrose Park; the clubhouse and tennis courts were demolished and replaced with residences in the 1920s.

A residents' association sprang up with the first houses, and the homeowners taxed themselves to provide gas streetlights in 1872, most of which are still standing. Montrose Park was not a distinct municipality; indeed it was part of the Village of South Orange, incorporated in 1869. But Montrose Park was perceived as a distinct place, and its residents were ready and able to support this illusion by supplying their own services. They established their own police patrol in the 1870s; even by 1890, when growth of the surrounding areas meant that the Village of South Orange needed to establish its own police department, the Village only paid for policemen during the day, so Montrose Park continued to collect funds to pay for a night patrol in their neighborhood. The restrictive covenants prohibited wires, so there was something of a delay in providing full electric and telephone service to the neighborhood, but with the development of underground conduits for service wires, Montrose Park was able to obtain the services it wanted while retaining the landscaped look its founder and residents cherished.

Thomas Alva Edison, the inventor of the light bulb and the man whose General Electric Company brought electricity and appliances to the homes of millions of Americans, lived and had his laboratory and some factories only a few miles from Montrose Park. The ability to light homes cleanly, reliably, and cheaply revolutionized domestic life. Queen Anne houses had big windows, to flood the interior with daylight, but come evening, the house could glow from within thanks to Mr. Edison's inventions.

Montrose Park became an idyllic place, as the trees lining the streets grew up, and the houses began to fill in. The first houses were in the popular mid-nineteenth century Franco-Italianate styles, but they were few and far between. The neighborhood became increasingly popular, and populated, in the 1880s and 90s, at the same time as the Queen Anne style became ascendant in American architecture. Montrose Park was a large subdivision, and in fact the majority of houses standing there today were not constructed until the early twentieth century. Thus, most houses in Montrose Park represent the popularity of the Colonial Revival and other Eclectic Revival styles of that time. As a buffer against all this residential development, the residents purchased additional land in 1908 to provide a public park, and they then spent even more money to have it landscaped. The park was turned over to the Village for the enjoyment of all, not just those in Montrose Park.

Montrose Park is today on the National Register of Historic Places as a historic district showcasing American domestic architecture of the last quarter of the nineteenth century and the first quarter of the twentieth. It includes 1,129 buildings, including residences, and the carriage houses and garages that were also constructed on the properties. Two of its many Queen Anne houses are showcased here to illustrate some of the varieties of the style. ✿

351 HARTFORD ROAD

IN 1894, JOHN G. FARON purchased a lot in Montrose Park, with the stipulation in his deed that "within one year erect upon this parcel of land a private dwelling house of the cost of at least six thousand five hundred dollars." The resulting fifteen-room brick house seems as solid today as it must have been when new. It is not a flamboyant example of the Queen Anne style, but it is a fine example nonetheless.

Homeowner credit and mortgages were in their infancy in the late nineteenth century, and the purchase of a lot and construction of a substantial house required considerable cash on hand. Faron, a young businessman, enlisted his whole family in the investment. Census records indicate that John Faron acted as the head of a household that included his mother and two brothers. The brothers were also employed in business, and the presumption is that they pooled their savings to bankroll this house. The Faron clan did live here for a few years after its construction, and then sold it. A tidy profit allowed John to purchase another house in the Montrose Park neighborhood, albeit one not quite so large. John Faron married, and he, his wife, and daughter remained in Montrose Park for many years.

The Faron House is solidly anchored to its broad, level lawns by a high brownstone foundation, rusticated after the Romanesque fashion. The exterior of the main portions of the house are executed in a hard-fired, machine-made brick, and the original joints were tinted red as well to give the masonry a solid, monolithic look. The third floor is marked by a high dormer with a large pediment above, all clad in gray slate, as is the hipped roof. The material aspect of the exterior is heavy, dark, and solid, and the broad porch rests on sturdy, simple columns. There is none of the delicate woodwork that gives so many American Queen Anne houses a lighthearted, festive look. But the broad, solid porch provides an enormous outside living space wrapping across the front and around the side of the house.

From the exterior, one almost does not realize how large the windows are, each boasting a large single pane of glass that announces, quietly, the technological advances of the age and the owner's wealth in securing these large panes for his house. The interior of the house is flooded with light from these large windows, and the layout insures that almost all rooms have windows on multiple elevations. The front entrance is through a double set of double doors, the outer ones delicately leaded and set into oak frames. This leads into the entry, with its tiled floor, and beveled glass panes in the interior doors bring light directly into the hall.

The living hall at the Faron House is typical for the Queen Anne style in that it contains the fireplace, the staircase, seating areas, and access to other parts of the house.

OPPOSITE: *The main staircase of the house at 351 Hartford Road, South Orange, New Jersey.*

Like many classic Queen Anne–style houses, this one focuses on a "living hall," a combination stairway, living room, reception room, and circulation space. The all-purpose nature of the space was intended to recall medieval "Great Halls" as part of the conscious historicism of the style. The classic living hall has a fireplace in it, although the size of the room and the presence of a staircase, which is open to the third floor, means that the fireplace alone would do very little to keep the living hall warm on a cold winter's day.

The stair railings and balusters are turned, extremely light and delicate in their appearance, and invite the eye and the occupant to travel up the stairs to a landing, where one can turn around and look down into the living hall, like a minstrel in a gallery. At the back of the living hall, a space has been screened from the main living hall by columns to form a library. Stained-glass windows showing the "lamp of wisdom" emphasize the use of the room, standing as they do above the bookshelves. From the living hall, smaller, distinct rooms are accessible, and can be separated from or integrated into the large central space by sliding pocket doors. This open and flexible floor plan is one of the most progressive elements of American architecture, developed both by the architects of the Shingle Style and by designers of Queen Anne houses during the latter nineteenth century.

Sliding pocket doors were a popular feature in many nineteenth-century homes.

OPPOSITE: Beamed ceilings were part of the effort to recreate a historical look in a new house, while the decorative wooden floors added to the richness of pattern found in a typical Queen Anne interior.

The Faron House was built with central heating, utilizing cast-iron radiators fired by the coal furnace in the basement. But as a design element, fireplaces, emphasizing the heart and hearth of the home, were important. Fireplaces appear in the first-floor living hall, the dining room, and in a second floor family sitting room and master bedroom. All were remodeled in the Colonial Revival style sometime in the twentieth century, but their location reveals an important aspect of the Queen Anne style. Although technologically fireplaces were obsolete, they were regarded as the most important symbolic part of a house, and were placed in rooms with strong symbolic associations.

As Clarence Cook, author of a popular book on interior decorating for the Queen Anne style house wrote, "Let us be glad of anything almost that keeps alive the sentiment of the fireplace, especially since we see how much has been done of late to re-instate the open fire in public favor. People have been finding out that though a furnace may be an excellent thing in the long-continued cold of winter, yet there are days in the early spring and late fall when a fire of logs is much pleasanter and seems to go more directly to the right spot."[40]

The Faron House has survived with few apparent alterations other than the replacement of original mantelpieces, and it remains in private ownership. No architect or pattern book has been identified as the source of the house's design, but it was certainly created by someone who was current on all the stylistic manifestations of the Queen Anne style. 🙢

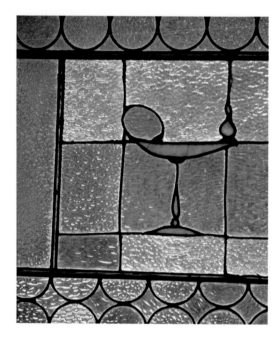

CLOCKWISE, BEGINNING WITH TOP LEFT: *Ornately decorated hardware sets the decorative tone at the front door; a detail of the colored and patterned tile used in the vestibule floor; the leaded glass window in the library features the lamp of wisdom; brick walls are set above a rusticated stone base with very thin mortar joints.*

OPPOSITE: *Four panel or five panel interior door configurations, such as used here, were a common form during the Queen Anne style.*

A FEW BLOCKS AWAY from the Faron House, another brick version of the Queen Anne style was built in Montrose Park. Builders in Montrose Park were, at least in the 1880s, to some degree imitating Bedford Park, a London suburb designed by English architect Richard Norman Shaw in the Queen Anne style. The self-conscious picturesqueness of Shaw's designs used brick and tile to simplify an Old English style for modern living, and in so doing, Shaw created a pleasant suburban neighborhood that immediately caught on with artists and writers as an expression of the latest in design. Bedford Park was a planned, landscaped suburb, begun in 1877, not unlike American examples such as Llewellyn Park which had been laid out decades earlier. But Bedford Park's use of the Queen Anne style for its speculative single-family and attached rowhouses helped to popularize the style for domestic use in England. Bedford Park was also widely noted in the American architectural press, both for its association with Shaw, one of the best-known English architects of the day, and for the design aspects of its layout.

A chirpy poem about Bedford Park, published in the London newspaper *St James' Gazette* in 1881, may never have been seen by any residents of Montrose Park, but the sentiments were probably shared by the indwellers of both "parks." Here is a portion of a much longer poem, perhaps one of the few in English to document the construction of a suburb:

The Ballad of Bedford Park
Here trees are green and bricks are red
And clean the face of man
We'll build our gardens here, he said
In the style of good Queen Anne.

Tis here a village I'll erect
With Norman Shaw's assistance
Where man will lead a chaste
Correct, aesthetical existence.[41]

The association of the suburbs with an improved, clean, and morally upright life was strong in the nineteenth century, and one vigorously upheld by the developers and promoters of suburban housing. The green trees and red bricks were certainly in evidence in several houses in Montrose Park, and "aesthetic" was the era's word of high praise for the eclectic architecture and decorating of the Queen Anne style.

The Taylor House in Montrose Park was built about 1887, on a brick base extending up from the foundation to incorporate the first floor, giving it the rosy color so desirable for the Queen Anne style on both sides of the Atlantic. The second floor is clad in wooden shingles, and the gables of the third floor are stucco and half-timber. A porch extends across the front and sides of the house, providing a shaded place to sit, and serving as a decorative device to balance the solid brick of the house walls.

An unusual period gas fixture illuminates and decorates the dining room.

OPPOSITE: *A bold fireplace with decorative relief tile was not part of the original construction but a sympathetic addition from the early twentieth century.*

Entering the Taylor House, one is immediately in the stair hall, a small room that is more hall than "living hall." From this hall one enters distinct front and rear parlors, a far more traditional floor plan than that found at the Faron House.

The house should more correctly be called the Taylor–Niebling House. The second owners of the house, the Neibling family, moved from Newark, New Jersey, to South Orange about 1912. They purchased the Taylors' house, and proceeded to renovate its principal rooms to reflect the Arts and Crafts sensibility then in vogue. The Queen Anne is aesthetically related to English Arts and Crafts in its origins, and the result is a pleasant harmony of styles.

The most dramatic intervention is in the living room, with its fireplace of green tiles rising high on the wall, and topped with a heavy oak beam. Likewise, the ceiling has been made more of a feature of the living room and dining room with the addition of wooden beams. Stained-glass windows add an almost medieval air to the room, perfectly in harmony with the taste of the English originators of the Arts and Crafts style. The bold, masculine look of the living room and dining room is held in counterpoint by the strikingly delicate, feminine decoration of the music room in the front of the house. This sort of radical distinction of interior spaces into divergent palettes, furniture type, and overall aesthetic was characteristic of Queen Anne architecture and decoration; its survival in a private house is quite rare after a century of modern decorators exhorting people to have rooms "flow" together and share decorative themes.

The light colors and forms of the music room décor contrast with the masculine design of the living room.

In the more private spaces of the house, the renovation of ca. 1912 did not obscure original, nineteenth-century finishes and features. For example in the back stair hall, extending from the kitchen up to the rear of the second floor, the original Lincrusta wall covering remains in place. Patented in England in 1887, Lincrusta was used as a sturdy, washable wall covering and was particularly popular in stairways and halls. It was intended as an imitation of tooled leather, but in its serviceable aspect, it was used in places where expensive pressed leather never would have been seen!

On the second floor, family bedrooms and sitting rooms retain a simplicity of form and function. The decorative excesses of the Queen Anne were usually overcome in bedrooms by the desire for serenity and cleanliness.

The overall effect of the Taylor–Neibling House is one of comfort, which was indeed one of the arguments for the Queen Anne style in its day. The house was designed and built to accommodate one of

LEFT: *A butler's pantry with original sink and cupboards is still a useful room.*

RIGHT: *The porch of a Queen Anne house was historically furnished during the warmer months with carpets, decorative wicker furniture, and decorative accessories like plants or lamps.*

the new technologies that revolutionized domestic life during the ascendancy of the Queen Anne style—the electric light. The present owner of the house is a knowledgeable collector of period lighting fixtures, and although none of the fixtures original to the house survive, the collection throughout the house showcases the splendid variety of lamps, chandeliers, and fittings available in the late nineteenth century. The house presently includes rare French flame-shaped bulbs in the dining room, on fixtures located at the crossing of the ceiling "beams." Another chandelier hangs down over the table. In the living room, or rear parlor, original table lamps provide a soft, warm glow that the Taylors and Nieblings would have recognized. 🏵

✿ LINCRUSTA ✿

IN AT LEAST TWO OF the houses shown in this chapter, an original wall covering survives. This durable material is Lincrusta, which was manufactured by the yard in the late nineteenth and early twentieth centuries. A complete installation is found in the Taylor House in South Orange, New Jersey. It serves as a sturdy, washable wall covering for the wainscot in the back staircase (shown in photo). Its use as a frieze in the dining room of the Conover House in Greenwich, Connecticut documents Lincrusta's use as a fine decorative finish as well.

Lincrusta was invented by Frederick Walton in 1877, an English linoleum-flooring manufacturer. It used similar materials to his flooring in order to create a wallcovering that could be embossed to form relief decoration. Lincrusta, his made-up name for the new product, is the combination of two Latin words: "linum," referring to the drying linseed oil used widely in traditional architectural finishes, and "crusta," meaning hard shell. The mixture of linseed oil, and a powder made of wood and plaster, was factory mixed and rolled.

The linseed oil made the material flexible enough so it could be stamped, molded, and otherwise patterned to create intricate, raised design. When dry, the Lincrusta, mounted on a paper backing, formed a semi-rigid material, usually sold in rolls like wallpaper, which was glued to walls and then finished in place.

Painted finishes would enhance the appearance of the Lincrusta and make it look like a plaster frieze, or a rich tooled leather wall covering. The variety of designs that could be produced cheaply and easily made Lincrusta a favorite in Queen Anne–style homes. Its relief and intricacy of design was perfect for the taste of the time, which emphasized a variety of patterns and textures both inside and outside the house.

Typically, Lincrusta was placed in stairways and vestibules, where the surface was both painted and varnished, making it easy to clean. It was also placed at cornices around rooms, where once painted, it was a good imitation of decorative plaster-work.

Although invented in England, several American companies soon copied the material and the process. Lincrusta was featured in the 1893 World Columbia Exposition in Chicago, as the product of American manufacturers. Lincrusta is still manufactured in England, and used by restorers today, both for its period appearance and its ability to hide cracks and uneven plaster walls.

Lincrusta wallcovering was often used in back stairs, as in this example from a house in South Orange, New Jersey.

PROSPECT STREET, MADISON, NEW JERSEY

IN CONTRAST TO THE planned suburban development of Montrose Park, where curvilinear streets were lined by custom-built houses, many more Queen Anne neighborhoods were created as expansions of existing communities. Such is the case in the town of Madison, New Jersey, a small village in the eighteenth century, which became part of the New York metropolitan region by the mid-nineteenth century with the extension of a railroad line through its rolling landscape. The area was quickly transformed from a farming community to a suburban one; the first daily commuter set off from Madison as early as 1840. He was joined by dozens, then hundreds, and today, thousands, who sought a pleasant home in a green setting an hour's commute away from midtown Manhattan.

By the 1880s some of Madison's entrepreneurs—a building contractor and the owner of a lumberyard—saw potential for housing the burgeoning numbers of commuters in a hillside lot extending up from the railroad station. The Cooks (builders) and the Smiths (lumberyard owners) got together to purchase the land and proceeded to subdivide it into 50 x 125 foot lots. They plotted lots on two existing streets, and laid out a third street between them, in order to provide as many lot fronts within easy walking distance of the train as possible. The new developers did not give their tract of land a fancy name, and they did not try anything innovative in street planning—the existing streets were part of a grid, and the new one fit right in.

Some of the houses were built for individual clients, but the Cooks, using the lumber from the nearby Smith & Pierson Lumber Yard, built many more speculatively. Speculative housing for a middle-class market was in high demand. For it to be a successful venture for Cook and Smith, it needed to be cheap, and to appeal to a broad variety of tastes. The developers chose to build houses in the Queen Anne style, using the plans of one of the mass-marketer architect/designers of the day, Robert W. Shoppell.

Shoppell led the Co-operative Building Plan Association, a New York firm that published a monthly magazine of domestic, and occasionally commercial, architectural designs. Shoppell and his stable of architects used the eclecticism of the era to promote, and indeed, help create the vernacular expression of the Queen Anne style for middle-class dwellings. Shoppell houses were usually wooden, in sizes and proportions intended to fit on the sort of lots like Cook and Smith were creating in Madison. The Shoppell houses could be built by American workmen from the prepared plans ordered through the mail; or, potential clients could write to the Co-operative Building Plan Association and ask for plans for a somewhat "customized" house.

By looking through the Shoppell-produced periodicals, it is possible to see that beginning in 1884, Cook and Smith used several of the published plans and designs as the source for building their speculative development in Madison. Several more houses in the neighborhood are similar to published designs, but not quite exact, suggesting that the builders modified existing plans for construction in their new neighborhood. Certainly they saved money by reusing plans within the neighborhood—different models reappeared on each street of the development. By changing the trim, or the color, or some other small details, the houses were prevented from looking exactly alike. No one ever complained; indeed, there was perhaps reassurance that these "new style" houses in a conservative small town were not completely unique.

Shoppell himself was sensitive to the fact that the Queen Anne style was new and perhaps somewhat alarming to traditionalists of the 1880s. In one of his publications, he noted:

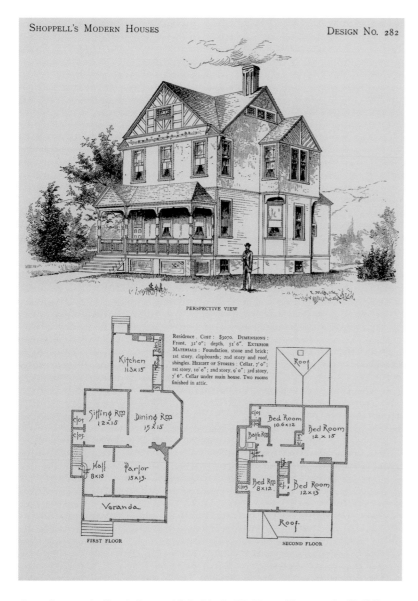

PERSPECTIVE VIEW

Residence. Cost : $3070. Dimensions :
Front, 31′ 0″; depth, 51′ 6″. Exterior
Materials : Foundation, stone and brick;
1st story, clapboards; 2nd story and roof,
shingles. Height of Stories : Cellar, 7′ 0″;
1st story, 10′ 0″; 2nd story, 9′ 0″; 3rd story,
7′ 6″. Cellar under main house. Two rooms
finished in attic.

FIRST FLOOR

SECOND FLOOR

One of many similar designs published in R. W. Shoppell's magazine Building
Designs *that form the basis of inspiration for the developer of the suburban
houses in Madison in the 1880s and 90s.*

Do not insist on having a very odd or a peculiar house; the owner himself is likely to tire of it, and if ever he is desirous of selling it, he will find a purchaser with difficulty. The best house is one whose exterior and interior are generally approved by people of good taste. On the other hand the house should not be too plain, such as a carpenter would design, for then it will be commonplace. It is believed that our publications are the most reliable guides in avoiding the extremes referred to.[42]

Like the other salesmen of mail-order plans, Shoppell produced plans for houses both modest and large. The houses erected speculatively in Madison, New Jersey are shown in the Shoppell publications of the 1880s as ranging from $2,000 to $4,000 to construct, making them squarely "middle class."

One of the houses Cook and Smith produced from Shoppell's plans stands today in a beautiful garden. The original owner purchased two lots side-by-side and built on one, perhaps planning to re-sell the other at a later date. But the double lot has remained attached to the house, providing a sweeping lawn and gardens that give this corner of the neighborhood a park-like feel.

The house itself seems to take its design from R. W. Shoppell's *Building Designs*, ca. 1890, and is entitled "Design No. 282." Like all his serial publications, an elevation drawing and floor plans were shown in the magazine; the builder then wrote to Shoppell's Co-operative Building Plan Association for a more complete set of plans. Design No. 282 included a porch across the front of the house, a bay window for the dining room, and a bathroom on the second floor—all the amenities required for comfortable modern life. In the Shoppell plate, the exterior is shown with half-timbering in the front-facing gable end, a detail that has been removed (or perhaps was never built). The published design is reversed, or presented in mirror image from the built example. This was a common phenomenon, where original drawings were copied onto plates, but after inking the copy, its form would reverse in the printing process.

Sometimes, houses were built purposefully as a mirror image of the plans, to take advantage of particular site conditions. Cook and Smith should have considered building Design 282 as shown in its illustration, rather than as reversed on the actual plans, for it would have allowed the dining room to open onto the garden side of the house's double lot, giving the room an attractive view.

The house has a rather simple and traditional plan, balancing the applied decorative touches of turned porch supports and shingle and wood siding. This sort of detail was used by Shoppell and others to project the image of style onto mass-market houses which were, in reality, still largely confined to a rectangular overall plan, in order to fit a 30' x 50' footprint on a rectangular lot. There was not much room for Shoppell houses and their like to open up and use the more open plans characterizing the style of larger houses.

But most of all, this house is about natural light. The first floor windows are relatively large, single-pane in both top and bottom sash, designed to give the clearest view and let in maximum light. The large windows are shown in the drawing with shades pulled nearly down; the current owner has installed wooden window shutters, which were also known and used in the Queen Anne style, to cut down on the ex-

Colored glass in the small-paned frame of this house is a surviving original detail.

treme brightness that penetrates the house on a clear day! The windows on the second floor of the house are enlivened with colored glass framing the main clear panel in the upper sash. The multi-colored effect is particularly notable from the exterior at night, when light from inside projects a cheerful glow outside—perhaps to gladden the hearts of the commuters, walking home on a dark winter's evening. During a sunny day, the colored glass glows within the house, making the occupant always aware of the motion of the sun. The multi-paned upper sash over a large, single-paned lower sash is typical of the Queen Anne style. The tiny panes in the front attic window are a medievalizing detail that adds interest to the façade, but without taking away light from the family's living quarters.

Unlike grander houses, this Queen Anne has only one staircase (plus a stair from the kitchen to the basement to facilitate getting food or equipment stored there). This was not a house to be run by servants, although the middle-class lady of the house might have had cleaning help come in and she may have "sent

Patterned "tin" or galvanized metal offered an inexpensive way to add much-loved pattern to an interior in a modest Queen Anne house such as this one.

out" some domestic chores such as laundry. The turned newel post of the stairs and the cascade of curved stairs at the bottom (seen in the floor plan), gave a graceful, but almost shorthand version of the living-hall staircase seen in the Watts Sherman House and other early examples of the style.

The interior rooms are also quite simple, and although historically their decoration may have involved more color, pattern, and texture than presently in vogue, their mantelpieces reflect a conservative taste among the builders and probably the original occupants of the house. The straight lines of the fireplace mantels could have come from designs of the Greek Revival and the 1830s. The small

Turned porch columns and jig-sawn cut wood detail enlivened the porches of almost all Queen Anne–style houses.

incised decoration in the parlor fireplace, with its rounded coal-grate opening, is the only nod to the Eastlake fashion of the 1870s and 80s. Pleasant and unostentatious, they remind us that not every Queen Anne–style house had a householder who embraced every aspect of the style.

Some details, like the decoratively patterned hardware, provide a glimpse of the more hyper-decorated state of many mass-produced products. The exterior surface of the house includes clapboard and shingles, to give the textural variety demanded of the style. The roof is now asphalt shingle, but would have been wooden when built, adding yet another texture, and quite likely, color, too, as wooden shingle roofs were painted, usually a dark red or brown. The house is presently painted in a modern, rather than historic color scheme, but the contrast of pale gray siding and white trim emphasizes the architectural lines.

The "development" created by Cook and Smith extended the town of Madison about 400 yards beyond the old downtown core, and extended the taste of its residents to an acceptance of late-Victorian architectural fashion. A few custom-built, grand Queen Anne–style houses were also built on the edges of Cook and Smiths' development, but the style is certainly concentrated in this area of town. Later, in the twentieth century, as other developers looked to create new neighborhoods, they selected the new, popular styles of their own eras—Bungalow, Colonial Revival, and the Split Level. The evidence of how Queen Anne came to town is clearly embodied in the pages of R. W. Shoppell's books of plans and designs, and the well-preserved neighborhood created with them. 🌸

HEMINGWAY HOUSE, OAK PARK, ILLINOIS

ERNEST MILLER HEMINGWAY, one of the great writers of the twentieth century, was born in Oak Park, Illinois, in 1899, in a house that epitomizes the Queen Anne style. Ernest Hemingway's maternal grandfather, Ernest Hall, had the house built around 1890, to designs by a local architect, Wesley Arnold. Grandfather Hall, born in England, had emigrated to the United States in the mid-nineteenth century, and made a modest fortune as the co-owner of a successful cutlery business in Chicago. He had this house built in the growing suburban community of Oak Park for his retirement years.

Grandfather Hall shared the house with his daughter, Grace Hall Hemingway, her husband, Dr. Clarence Hemingway, and their growing family. Ernest was the second of six children born to Grace and Clarence, four of whom were delivered by their father in this house. Their cries and bustle must have been just the thing to fill the house for widower Grandfather Hall, but on his death in 1905, young Ernest Hemingway and his family left this house for a new one, also in Oak Park, one that reflected the Prairie-style design ideas first presented by another local architect, Frank Lloyd Wright. The family's conscious seeking of modernity and its move away from the nineteenth-century house may have instilled in young Ernest the desire to seek modernity in his fiction writing, but the author's roots, personally and professionally, may still be traced to the late Victorian era.

Hemingway's working life began as a newspaper correspondent, but he is best known for stories of adventure and a sharp realism of observation and plot. *For Whom the Bell Tolls*, *The Old Man and the Sea*, and other works have become classics of American literature. Ernest Hemingway won the Nobel Prize for Literature in 1954. In 1961, he ended his own life, just as his father had many years before, with a self-inflicted gunshot. Ernest Hemingway never came back to this childhood home, preferring a life of adventure in France, Spain, Cuba, Africa, and the American West, but it is tempting to think that such an adventurous spirit was able to flourish because of the deep, stable roots he put down growing up in Oak Park, Illinois.

The Hemingway House is located midblock on a broad street just beyond the downtown commercial center of Oak Park. The neighborhood includes several late nineteenth-century-frame residential structures, spanning the popular stylistic vocabularies of the era, including Queen Anne, Shingle Style, Gothic Revival, Romanesque Revival, and Classical Revival. The Hemingway House is typical of the American Queen Anne style, built entirely of wood, its elevations characterized by asymmetry. The form of the house is based on an L shape, putting enclosed gable ends on the front and side, and the corner of the L is filled in with a conical-roofed turret. The turret extends the height of the house, creating rounded corners in the front parlor on the first floor and best bedroom on the second floor. This sort of plan which "breaks the box" of traditional room configurations is one of the incipient "modern" features of the Queen Anne style.

A porch wraps across the front and side of the first floor of the house, its spindly supports and railings turned on a machine-driven lath. A broad flight of wooden stairs rises on the far side of the porch, leading directly to a pair of double front doors. The oak doors, finished with a varnish rather than painted, represented the height of fashion for the 1890s. The warm glow of the woodwork is set off by elaborately decorative hardware for the doorknob and doorbell. The off-center entry location on the façade is emphasized by broad stairs leading to it; the wide double front door visually balances the turret on the other side of the house. The house is finished with clapboard, using decorative fish-scale shingles as an accent in the pedimented gables and on the top of the turret. Currently painted in modest shades of gray, the house's exterior does not reflect the more vivid colors often associated with the Queen Anne style, but reminds us that then, as now, individual taste did not always conform to that promoted by contemporary tastemakers.

Windows are large, with single clear panes of glass, allowing light to pour into the interior. The concern for light and air in the late-Victorian era cannot be overstated, and this house fully incorporated all the modern thinking of the day in providing cross-ventilation within the house, full lighting, both natural and from gas fixtures, and sanitary plumbing to bring fresh water in and to take away waste.

The first-floor parlor, in the base of the turret, includes a prominent decorative element in the fireplace. By the Queen Anne era, fireplaces were obsolete as a source of heating, but they continued to be built, and highly decorated, as the symbolic "heart and hearth" of the home. The Hemingway House has decorative mantels in both the parlor and dining room. They are both typical factory-produced models, although certainly at the upper range of cost due to the applied carvings, built-in bevel-edged mirror, and tiles applied around the fireplace opening.

Both mantels very nearly match the description of a fireplace mantel in *Hints on Household Taste* by Charles Eastlake. Eastlake was an English decorator and writer, perhaps the most influential voice in interior decoration and furnishings in the last quarter of the nineteenth century. His book, first published in England in 1868, reached American shores at the same time the Queen Anne style of architecture was being introduced. This little book of advice on everything from floor coverings, wallpapers, curtains, furniture, and metalwork, went to four editions, and remained very popular for years on both sides of the Atlantic. Eastlake wrote of libraries:

> Few men care for a mirror in such a room; but if it is indispensable to the mantel-piece, let it be a long low strip of glass, stretching across the width of the chimney-breast, about eighteen inches in height...Over this may be raised a capital set of narrow shelves—for specimens of old china, &c....A little museum may thus be formed, and remain a source of lasting pleasure to its possessors, seeing that 'a thing of beauty is a joy forever.[43]

The parlor of the Hemingway House is presented today with decorative china, busts of Lincoln and Mozart, and a family photograph—the perfect "little museum" reflected in the overmantel mirror that Eastlake proposed. The dining-room mantel is similarly adorned with china, silver, and at the very top, plates set behind a plate rail of delicately turned spindles, a miniature version of a Queen Anne porch railing. Period photographs of many Queen Anne interiors confirm that the fireplace mantel remained a center for decorative display in American homes through the early 1900s, and that many in principal rooms incorporated shelves and mirrors.

Eastlake may have recommended the fireplace shelves form a "museum" display, but he could not have anticipated that in the third-floor turret room, Dr. Hemingway is said to have literally kept his own natural history museum—his collection of mounted and preserved wildlife. Dr. Hemingway instilled in his son Ernest a love of the outdoors, which began with walks through the woods just beyond Oak Park, and lasted throughout the adult writer's career.

The Hemingway House also has its own library, lined with bookshelves and portraits of family members. Both the parlor and library have wall-to-wall floral carpeting, a popular floor treatment for the late-Victorian era. Decorative plasterwork in the coved cornice was created with applied, mass-produced pieces, put together to create a look of custom interior design. The layers of decorative detail—in the

The fireplace became a center for decoration and display in the Queen Anne style, both in the architecture and the ornaments displayed on and around it.

cornice, on multiple wallpapers, on floor carpet, in furniture and window treatments—represent the fashionable aesthetic of the period. The rich variety of materials, colors, and textures shown in even one room represents the outpouring of a new manufacturing economy, one which brought former luxury goods to a broad swath of the population.

If the parlor, dining room, and library represent the culmination of centuries of decorative detail, the kitchen and bathroom represent the avant-garde of the technological American home. The Hemingway House was built with a kitchen intended to be staffed by servants, and the back stairs led directly up from the kitchen to the servants' own rooms on the second floor. But the servants' lot was made considerably easier in this typical Queen Anne house than it might have been in earlier eras. The kitchen included a porcelain-enameled sink on legs, which made it possible to wash dishes and fill buckets without pumping water, stooping over a tub on the floor, or carrying waste water outside to dump. Varnished oak wainscot lined the room, creating an easy-to-clean surface. The big coal stove with its nickel-plate accents not only looks sleek and efficient, compared to older, bulky coal stoves, but it was arranged to have cooking surfaces, ovens, and warming shelves, facilitating various cooking methods. A large oak dresser held plates,

Back stairs leading directly to the kitchen signaled that the house was intended to be operated with the help of servants; at least one lived with the Hemingways during the years they occupied the house.

Domestic technology had advanced considerably during the nineteenth century so that by the 1890s, the elements of a modern kitchen—stove with oven, sink with hot and cold running water, food preparation area, and icebox (not visible in photo) were all assembled into one room.

cutlery, and glassware inside drawers and glass-fronted cupboards, again keeping housewares clean between uses. A center work table is even illuminated by an overhead light. The move of artificial light sources out of the parlor alone and into service areas was a testament to the growing technological sophistication of American homes, and the declining price of light fixtures and their fuel sources.

The second floor of the Hemingway House held six bedrooms and the only bathroom in the house. Its tub, sink, and toilet further expressed the interest in hygienic, efficient living so popular in the late nineteenth century. Bedroom furnishings included white enameled bedsteads, which were considered "hygienic" and marketed as more healthful than ornate carved wooden bed frames that caught dust and discouraged air flow.

As was common for the period, Mr. and Mrs. Hemingway had separate bedrooms. Grace's room has been restored most accurately, using a surviving fragment of original wallpaper to inform the restoration of the floral patterned room. Another nineteenth-century book of decorating advice by Clarence Cook, a rival in print to Charles Eastlake, had this to say about bedrooms:

Grace Hemingway's bedroom, flooded with light from the turret windows.

What pleasant places our mothers' bedrooms used to be! In the old time American formal and pretentious way of living, …it was good that there was one room in the house where domestic feeling was allowed a chance to root itself at ease…. No parlor, however free to let its luxuries or simple elegance be enjoyed…can take the place, I think, of the "mothers bedroom," which still exists, I hope, as of old, in many and many a home. [44]

The house has a stiffness, a verticality in its appearance that puts it squarely in the realm of the vernacular building tradition. But it was a comfortable house, and its decorative and technological elements make it an outstanding example of the Queen Anne style of American architecture. Its architect, Wesley Arnold, was a local man, of whom too little is known. Like most other small-town architect-builders of his time, he was probably largely self-taught in his trade. Census records place him in Cook County, Illinois in 1880, where as a young man of twenty-nine he lived with his cousin, Frederick Arnold, and his family. Frederick was also a carpenter. Wesley had been born in New York, but seems to have moved to

The Hemingway children's nursery. The painted-iron beds came into fashion during this time and were believed to be more sanitary than wooden bed frames.

Illinois to be with family and to learn a trade, and he found a ready market in the booming suburb of Oak Park. He was ready to provide to a self-made client, Mr. Hall, the latest in popular design, despite the fact that in 1890, when the house was built, the Eastern architectural establishment was promoting neo-classicism and the Colonial Revival style as the only suitable design for domestic architecture. The Hemingway House is utterly typical of many across America, and it asserts the broad popularity and practicality of the Queen Anne for the house-building public.

Because of its association with the Nobel–Prize winning author, 339 North Oak Park Avenue, in the Chicago suburb of Oak Park, Illinois, was preserved, thus keeping a typical example of American Queen Anne architecture from the turn of the twentieth century as a furnished house museum. The Ernest Hemingway Birthplace is open to the public, operated by a private, nonprofit organization that is committed to the preservation of the house and to commemorating Hemingway's associations with the community of Oak Park. 🌀

PARKER HOUSE, OAK PARK, ILLINOIS

FRANK LLOYD WRIGHT (1867–1959) is certainly, in popular understanding, at least, the most famous architect in American history. Wright's long career went from the Victorian era to the Atomic Age, but his work was always a step ahead of everyone else, so that many of his buildings remain startlingly modern today.

Frank Lloyd Wright's interest in design was evident from an early age, and the story goes that his mother had determined from his birth that he would become an architect. Wright took some mechanical drawing and mathematics courses at the University of Wisconsin, but he never earned a college degree, and certainly had no formal architectural training such as was being instituted at Eastern schools like M.I.T., Cornell, and Columbia in the 1870s and 80s. Instead, Wright learned architecture in the traditional way, by working as an apprentice, learning the craft and the business from an established practitioner. When he was twenty, Wright left his home in Wisconsin and went to the booming city of Chicago, where he found work as a draftsman's apprentice for Joseph Lyman Silsbee (1843–1913).

Silsbee was from an old New England family, and was academically trained, first as an undergraduate at Harvard, and then at M.I.T. He studied there in 1870, the year of the architecture school's founding. Silsbee went on to work for Boston architectural firms, and he was one of the rare Americans with architectural training who traveled to Europe in the 1870s. His interest in architecture led him to seek out Richard Norman Shaw, the leading architect of the Queen Anne Revival in England. On his return to the States, Silsbee set up practice in Syracuse, and later (in 1882) in Buffalo, New York, where he specialized in houses in the Queen Anne and Shingle styles.

In 1886, Silsbee went to Chicago, where he opened an architectural practice with a colleague from Buffalo, Edward Kent. The firm of Silsbee & Kent developed a thriving practice very quickly in the rapidly growing city and its suburbs, and soon hired young architects and apprentices to help them produce the houses, churches, and civic buildings that were commissioned. In addition to Frank Lloyd Wright, Silsbee & Kent also gave a professional start to others who would become outstanding architects, including George Grant Elmslie, George Maher, and Irving Gill.

Wright left Silsbee's office in 1888 to work for another Chicago firm, Adler and Sullivan. Louis Sullivan, the design partner, was always remembered fondly by Wright as his mentor and the primary influence on his professional development. Dankmar Adler was an engineer. When Wright joined their office, Adler & Sullivan were in the midst of designing the Auditorium Building, an impressive Romanesque Revival–style building with an acoustically and structurally challenging auditorium/concert hall inside. The successful merger of innovative design with technical brilliance earned the firm accolades, and built Chicago's already considerable reputation as the center of innovation in American architecture in the 1880s and 90s.

Adler & Sullivan taught Wright about buildings of larger scale and substance rather than residences. Sullivan urged examination of buildings for their essential geometric form, and tried in his work to make clear massing to be a dominant feature of expression. Sullivan is today known for the sinuous, Celtic or Art Nouveau-inspired ornamentation that decorated his buildings, but the decoration was always applied as an enrichment of underlying geometry, and never obscured the basic form of the building.

Wright married in 1889, and borrowed money from Sullivan to put a down payment on a lot in suburban Oak Park, Illinois. A short train ride away from downtown Chicago, yet a village with tree-shaded streets and wide building lots, Oak Park was developing as a suburban community for the professionals and managers who kept business in The Loop humming. Wright built a house for himself and his bride, and

The large windows in the turret of the house, placed side-by-side, open up the interior to the light and forecast the horizontal lines of Wright's Prairie Style.

OPPOSITE: *In Wright's hands, the main staircase incorporates the turned staircase, spindle railings, and paneling of the Queen Anne style to create a more modern, rather than historical, effect.*

soon they had children. They would have six in all, from 1890 to 1903, with the attendant need for clothing, toys, and music lessons—all the things an upwardly mobile family in Oak Park in the 1890s would want for their offspring. Frank Lloyd Wright felt the financial pinch, and in addition to his job at Adler & Sullivan, he began accepting commissions on his own to design houses for neighbors and friends in Oak Park.

Adler & Sullivan had warned him not to strike out on his own like that; insisting that all work Wright produced should be run through the firm. But Wright did it anyway; in 1892 he accepted a commission to design a series of three houses for Thomas H. Gale on lots just a few blocks west of Wright's own home on Chicago Avenue in Oak Park. The commission was found out by Adler & Sullivan, which led to Wright's departure from the firm to go into business on his own. He added a studio/workspace onto his home, and set to work on his own practice, thereby accelerating the development of his own style, now known as the Prairie Style.

The master bedroom seems to float in the treetops.

Innovative ideas are never completely divorced from what came before, however. In the houses commissioned by realtor Thomas Gale in Oak Park in 1892, one sees an architectural snapshot of the first steps Frank Lloyd Wright took toward developing his Prairie Style residences. The houses remain firmly grounded in the popular Queen Anne style he had learned from his first employer, Joseph Silsbee, yet bear the mark of Sullivan's insistence on geometric clarity. All three of the Gale houses on Chicago Avenue remain standing today.

Robert P. Parker was a Chicago attorney, typical of the professionals who lived in Oak Park. Gale had the houses built on speculation; one he lived in himself, and the other two were sold. The Robert P. Parker House is one of these "Bootleg Houses," a term Wright later applied to them, acknowledging their design on time stolen, or "bootlegged" from his employer, Adler & Sullivan.

The Parker House is a roughly square plan house, sited in a standard suburban lot of about 50 feet by 150 feet. The square mass is controlled and finished by the prominent hipped roof, which shelters the house rather like an oversized hat, and the roof line extends well beyond the walls, as if the "hat" were pulled down over one's ears. Although a full three-story house, including an attic, the roof is extended down so that the eaves are at the top of the first floor. This visible expression of shelter was important in Frank Lloyd Wright's Prairie Style work, creating the appearance of a low cozy house form, although in height and bulk the houses are sized similarly to neighboring buildings of more traditional styles.

The Parker House is not simply a square with a big peaked roof, however. Like other Queen Anne–style houses, there are dormer windows, and prominent corner turrets that break out of the mass of the main block front and back. The turrets are octagonal, and thus expressive of the wooden construction of the building. The geometric masses of each part of the house—square, octagon, cone (the turret roof)—are clearly visible, in a way that reflects the influence of Sullivan on Wright.

These geometric extensions provide prominent window locations as well, bringing light into the house. The typical Queen Anne window of a large sheet of glass bordered with small panes has been simplified in the projecting turrets of the first floor to become a fixed sheet of plate glass and a border almost reminiscent of book design in the late nineteenth century. A more standard Queen Anne house may have filled the openings with a group of traditional, vertically oriented windows, but Wright's single panes are horizontal in orientation. This forecasts more than anything the horizontal linearity and orientation that came to dominate the Prairie Style.

On the second floor, the windows in the turrets are smaller, operable casements, and the design has a stronger vertical influence. But enclosed as they are in a continuous band of molding top and bottom, and set under the deep eaves, the overall impression is of a horizontal line of windows.

A newly renovated kitchen maintains the materials and spirit of a modern suburban house of the 1890s.

Under the eave line of the main roof is a plain frieze band, which wraps around the entire house creating a firm line around the midsection of the house, and delineating the clear break between first and second floors. The horizontal, open effect of the house is further enhanced by the use of terraces, rather than roofed porches, at the front entry and off the dining room. The dining terrace lets light into the house through the glass doors that lead to it. Edged with low walls, the dining terrace continues a horizontal line around the house that unites front and back turrets. The dining terrace is screened from a view of the street, and positioned so that in summer trees will shade it, but with the leaves down, it provides a sunny, sheltered place to enjoy some fresh air and laugh at the long Chicago winter.

The front entry terrace is also surrounded by a solid wall of shingles, and breached by a flight of stairs that narrows as it approaches the top. Throughout his life, Wright's work was characterized by sheltered, even hidden entrances, as if the house were a castle protecting its occupants from entry and attack by the outside world. In the Parker House, the main entry is clearly visible from the street, with a walkway from the public sidewalk leading right up to it, but the narrowing of the stairs, the high terrace wall, and the solid front door send a message that entry to the house is guarded. These design elements also play with the expected Queen Anne device of a broad stair leading to a covered porch, with open railings and spindles drawing the eye and footsteps of the visitor to the front entry, which frequently had a window or glass pane installed in it. Wright could only begin to depart from the standard architectural conventions of the day had he not known them so well.

Immediately beside the front door is a window that gives light into the entrance hall and affords a view of those who might approach the house.

The entrance hall is dominated by the main staircase, with a delicate screen of spindles providing a decorative way of partially obscuring the upper stairs leading to the private family quarters, and allowing light to filter into the hall from a side window, or at night, from the built-in light fixture on the stair. The location of the staircase and the placement of windows and light fixtures in it are perfectly typical of the Queen Anne style. Later in his career, Wright would minimize the staircases in his houses, enclosing them within the core of a house. Perhaps his most memorable treatment of the change of level within a building was the design of the circular ramps inside the Guggenheim Museum in New York, his last work. But at the Parker House, Wright is still working in the standard Queen Anne formula of an open stair in the entrance hall, but it is beautifully clean-lined. A built-in bench fills in the corner of the L formed by the stairs. Built-in benches and bookshelves had emerged in the Queen Anne period as standard features for a middle-class home. Wright would later make built-ins a hallmark of his work but here the hall bench is largely conventional in its design and placement.

From the hall, one enters the large and bright living room, an irregular space that includes the semi-octagon at the base of the front turret. The large windows flood the room with light, and make for an inviting seating area. Further into the room lies the fireplace, set on an angle in the corner with its massive brick front and relatively small hearth opening. The placement of the fireplace is typical of Queen Anne–style houses, and does not foretell Wright's Prairie Style devise of placing the fireplace in its own alcove or inglenook. But the large expanse of raw brick does have a distinctly Wrightian flavor. More typical Queen Anne–style fireplaces would have covered much of the fireplace with wood paneling, tile, or a more decorative brick and stone.

The dining room occupies part of the rear turret, and so has wraparound windows affording views of the garden and filling the room with light. The woodwork throughout the first floor of the house is finished in a deep-toned stain and varnish, again, a feature quite typical for Queen Anne houses of the 1890s. In Wright's hands, however, dark woodwork served to establish a strong horizontal line in the interior spaces. This horizontal is perhaps another precursor of the Prairie Style, particularly seen in the dark line of the picture railing running around the room at about 7/8 of a foot up the wall, set against the warm yellows, terra-cottas, and off-whites that he favored.

Upstairs, this family house has three bedrooms, and now two baths, although originally built with just one. The bedrooms lying in the turrets are airy, light-filled spaces. The master bedroom has a fireplace with tile-faced mantle, using tiles typical of the period, green with amber-yellow streaks. The fireplace in the bedroom is a decorative element, for the large radiators installed in the room attest to the fact that the 1890s builders understood that the beautiful large windows would create drafty, cold conditions in winter.

The third floor, under that steeply sloping roof, has been remodeled in the late twentieth century to include a playroom and home office. When it was built, the upstairs would have been storage, and perhaps contained a room for a live-in servant. The house is not large; rather it is a comfortable single-family home for a "modern" middle-class suburban family of the 1890s, and it still serves that role well. However, in the 1890s, such a family would more likely than not have a live-in servant to take care of household cleaning, washing, and cooking.

The Robert P. Parker House is intriguing as one particular architect's personal interpretation of the Queen Anne style. Because of his youth and talent, it also offers a vision of where Frank Lloyd Wright's architectural career would go. Wright's work in the Prairie Style evolved in Oak Park, and today the village remains the densest concentration of Frank Lloyd Wright's architecture in the world. The Parker House, and its neighboring "Bootleg Houses" are among Wright's earliest work in Oak Park, and so document the development of his unique Prairie Style from more common Queen Anne–style origins. 🐚

Queen Anne style influenced Wright in the division of the windows into a large center pane surrounded by smaller panes on the margin, although he pushed the design into a new aesthetic through his refusal to be bound by the conventions of the time.

WILLIAM E. CONOVER HOUSE, GREENWICH, CONNECTICUT

BUILT IN 1888 on a hilly piece of land extending into Long Island Sound, William Conover's house is a wonderful example of the Queen Anne style, as interpreted by architect Oscar Teale. The area was called "Belle Haven" and was promoted in the 1880s and 90s as a desirable residential neighborhood, within an easy carriage drive of downtown Greenwich, Connecticut, and its railroad connections to New York and New Haven.

The house was published in May 1890 in *Scientific American Architects and Builder's Edition*. The weekly *Scientific American* magazine introduced a monthly edition devoted exclusively to architecture and building technology in the 1880s. The magazine emphasized domestic architecture and ran illustrations and plans for both modest and more lavish homes. The intent of the magazine was to drum up business for mail-order plans offered through the magazine's in-house architects at their offices in New York, and it stated that "hundreds of dwellings have already been erected on the various plans we have issued, and many others are in the process of construction."[45]

But *Scientific American's Builder's Edition* also served to form the taste of the American public. By presenting new fashions in domestic architecture through a popular magazine that reached an audience of potential homebuilders and buyers, not just architects, it helped Americans to accept not just the technology but the aesthetics of the era. And the era of *Scientific American Architects and Builders Edition* was dominated by the Queen Anne style, so it is not surprising that the magazine showcased it, particularly in its domestic, middle-class expression.

The Conover House was one of the houses that were published in the magazine as what the editors would have called "a most interesting example of modern architectural construction." The description of the Conover House was typical for the magazine's featured houses, and it reads as a cross between a practical real estate enumeration of features and a breathless listing of the elements a late nineteenth-century- American audience would find desirable in a home.

"A Residence at Belle Haven, Conn."
We reproduce…an excellent design of a country house recently completed for Mr. W. E. Conover, at Belle Haven, Conn. It contains five, large rooms elegantly furnished, and a broad, pleasant piazza. The framework throughout is sheathed and covered with shingles, stained a dark green; the roof moss green. Dimensions: Front 42 ft., sides 51 ft., not including piazzas. The entrance is through a vestibule, with Dutch doors of antique oak, and provided with a staircase of unusual beauty, having bits of carving, spindle screens, etc. This hall has a large, open fireplace, handsomely furnished with a hearth laid with rich tiling, a hard wood mantel; the other fireplaces are fitted up in similar style…The drawing room is trimmed with cherry, the library with

This detail of the porte cochere shows the Roman brick used at its base.

mahogany, and the dining room with oak. The kitchen and pantries are wainscoted and trimmed with whitewood, finished in the natural. There are five large bedrooms on [the] second floor, well lighted and provided with ample closets. There is also a bathroom, wainscoted, and containing tub, bowl and water closet, all complete. The plumbing is of the best. There are two bed rooms, store room, and billiard room in the attic. There is a cemented cellar under [the] whole of the house, containing laundry and furnace. The house is furnished with electric bells, speaking tubes, gas, and all the modern improvements. Cost $14,250.
    OSCAR S. TEALE, of New York, architect.

Conover was one of the first residents of the area, and his house must have served as an advertisement to convince others to build in the neighborhood, too. The published price put it, in 1890, in the realm of exclusive housing, aimed at the prosperous upper-middle class. Although for the most part a neighborhood of full-time residents, Belle Haven's socially conscious inhabitants took their architectural cues from the New England summer resort communities of Newport, Rhode Island, and Mt. Desert, Maine. Like these places, Belle Haven soon boasted several Shingle Style–houses of considerable size. The Shingle Style was the high-style expression of domestic architecture in the 1880s, and more likely to be designed by formally trained architects, and less likely to be published in popular magazines like *Scientific American*. Hence the exuberant Queen Anne house built for Conover in 1888 soon became something of an architectural anomaly in its neighborhood, and it is no surprise that by 1910 the house was extensively remodeled.

Outside, the Conover House was remade to show more references to classicism consistent with the taste of the early twentieth century. The Conover House originally had a porch and porte cochere, and these were retained in 1910, but rebuilt with sturdier lines. The 1888 version of the house had the typical turned porch supports of the day that produced an effect that was light and delicate and entirely innovative. The current version of the house features thick Doric columns along the porch, and the porch railing transformed to a classical balustrade, although executed in wood just like the more sticklike arrangement of the earlier version of the house.

The dining-room fireplace with tiled hearth and mantel incorporates a shelf for decorative displays of ceramics or antique cookware.

The base of the porte cochere was also enhanced, being rebuilt in newly fashionable Roman brick. With a face longer and narrower than conventional brick, Roman brick gave a decidedly horizontal emphasis to walls. It was not exactly Roman, but its name associated it with classical architecture and a two-thousand-year-old tradition of building. Roman brick was generally produced in a warm ochre- to rust-colored palette, speckled with black, not the flat red of common brick. The color was played up at the Conover House with red-tinted mortar; indeed white and off-white mortars were avoided throughout the last third of the nineteenth century and into the early twentieth century and considered inappropriate. The idea was to treat the masonry wall as a single unit, with color correspondence between stone and mortar or brick and mortar, and those colors in turn to be picked up in the painted body of the house.

In another example of the mason's art typical of the Queen Anne style, the chimneys at the Conover House are highly decorative, with patterns of banding and corbelling enlivening their tall surface. The chimneys serve to punctuate the irregular floor plan, which, with its angled bay windows, appears to pivot around a center held firm by the great chimneys. The wraparound porch now extends to an angled wing, added in 1910, which was a large screened room, taking advantage of summer breezes from off the Sound. Later development and the growth of trees and shrubs have now obscured the house's views of the water, or of distant views of the countryside to the north.

The 1910 alteration extended the original idea of projecting bays from each corner of the house. The irregularity of the building's footprint and profile are inescapable elements of the Queen Anne style, which wanted, above all, to avoid the conformity of boxlike rooms in boxlike houses that ignored the benefits of light and air. The late Victorians knew that a well-sited window or door could bring health benefits as well as a playful quality to a house, and they celebrated the opportunity to vary the surface of a wall with a projecting bay window or extended gable. Thus, the front corners of the Conover House open up as bays with paired windows, projecting past the body of the house under a gable on one side and a turret on the other. The lack of symmetry for the façade is completely in character with the Queen Anne style, and the

A RESIDENCE AT BELLE HAVEN, CONN.—[See page 79.]

The Conover House by Oscar Teale was published shortly after its construction. Remodeling two decades later extended the house with an addition off the dining room and across the rear of the house.

Above the wood-paneled walls in the dining room, painted and glazed Lincrusta decorates the room's frieze.

fact that it was not changed in the 1910 remodeling suggests how the Conovers found the interior spaces thus created both charming and useful.

With this theme of utilizing natural light, it is therefore unusual to find that the stairs were located in the interior of the Conover House. It is far more common the have the stairs on an outside wall, lighted by a large and decorative window or punctuated by stained-glass windows casting a warm glow on the stairs in daylight hours. The Conover House stairs are instead lighted by interior windows, which transmit some light from an outside window across a hallway. This is more technically innovative than practical, and speaks more to the capability of the original designer than to any design trend for the style. More lighting is provided over the main stairs by an enormous chandelier, not original to the house but quite in keeping with its character. The Conover House was originally designed to use gas lighting, and later converted to electricity.

But the Conovers did not adopt change simply for its own sake. Long after electricity arrived and began to power stoves and other kitchen appliances, the family kept the original stove, and surprisingly, so did all the subsequent owners. No longer in use, the "Perfect" stove is still ensconced in the fireplace wall the way most stoves were in the late nineteenth century, using the masonry chimney to vent the great cast-iron stove, fueled by buckets of coal.

The dining room and kitchen and service areas were extended in 1910, although the decorative vocabulary for the dining room would remain dominated by the fireplace, with its green-tiled firebox framed by a massive wooden mantel. The paneled walls of the dining room do not extend all the way to the ceiling, leaving room for a deep decorative frieze, filled in this case with a delicately painted Lincrusta wallcovering.

The use of a wide frieze as an area for decorative borders, most often in a dining room, has its

The porch of the Conover House, like many Queen Anne houses, provides a comfortable indoor-outdoor space.

origins in the English Arts and Crafts movement and was used in American Queen Anne houses as well as Craftsman–style houses, giving it a popularity from the 1880s through the 1920s. Also within the dining room, the introduction of electricity was celebrated in 1910 with the installation of multiple bare-bulb fixtures, one at each crossing of a faux-Tudor beamed ceiling. The inherent eclecticism was perfectly in keeping with the late nineteenth-century's attitude toward historic architecture as a set of distinct design elements to be mined and freely used, unbound by conventions of "historically correct" use or burdened with the desire to recreate a physically authentic environment of an earlier time. It was the spirit of the past that informed the designers and renovators of a house like William Conover built, combined with a practicality at incorporating technologies and systems that worked to make the house comfortable.

The coexistence of the earlier fireplace along with added ceiling beams and lighting in the dining room attest to how the Conovers kept many elements of the 1888 house and enhanced them, in the process extending the architectural vocabulary of the Queen Anne style to gracefully blend it with more avant-garde tastes of 1910, including Craftsman Style, Colonial Revival, and Tudor Revival elements. The renovation, which formed much of the house we see today, offers a good look at the changes and continuity of Queen Anne style from the height of its popularity to its last expression. 🏵

URBAN HOUSES

THE RAMBLING FLOOR PLANS and propensity toward the use of wood in the American expression of the Queen Anne style made it a difficult choice in urban settings.

The two examples that follow are located in major American cities, but both were originally located far enough away from downtown so as to have had a small yard around them. The Haas–Lilienthal House survived the San Francisco earthquake of 1906 and then the total rearrangement of its neighborhood, from a fashionable area of single-family homes to the periphery of a commercial center. It is now a museum and one of the outstanding West Coast examples of the Queen Anne style inside and out.

The Beeson House, constructed in the city of Chicago, uses a combination of motifs that brings it close to the English antecedents of American Queen Anne, but its materials, local limestone and wood, make it clearly a Chicago expression of the style.

In parts of New York City and Boston, and in some other East Coast cities, there were masonry houses erected in the 1870s and early 1880s that took their design cues from the English Queen Anne style. The English Queen Anne was notable for the use of brick with limestone trim (or wood painted to look like stone) and an architectural vocabulary that employed the classical forms that were actually in use during the reign of Queen Anne in England (1702–1714). Quoins, curvy pediments, and urns were popular motifs. An early example of the type, built in Boston, was published in *American Architect and Building News* in 1879. The house is part of a spectacular row of similarly-styled townhouses in the Back Bay section of the city; its exterior remains today, but its interior has been carved into several apartments.

The urban Queen Anne townhouse exists, but it is a very small percentage of American houses in the style. The English-derived materials and detailing shown on this published townhouse did not influence other nonurban houses, or indeed, any other urban buildings. Many more urban Queen Anne houses exist as freestanding examples, set closely together on the narrow urban lots that characterized the era's new developments.

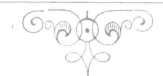

HAAS–LILIENTHAL HOUSE, SAN FRANCISCO, CALIFORNIA

DURING THE FRIGHTENING MORNING hours of April 18, 1906, the residents of the city of San Francisco, California, realized that it was not only the shaking of the earth that would destroy their city, but also the subsequent fires that erupted from broken gas mains and upended coal stoves. Van Ness Avenue, a wide boulevard that had been laid out as a setting for spacious lots of expensive, beautiful residences, was chosen by city leaders as a firebreak, and the houses along it were purposely destroyed by dynamite so that many other buildings and people might survive.

So it was that the Haas–Lilienthal House, built one block to the west of Van Ness Avenue on quieter Franklin Street, was saved from the calamities of the Great San Francisco Earthquake, and in the process became a rare survivor of the Gilded Age mansions that had once marked this corner of the city. Built in 1886 at the height of the popularity of the Queen Anne style, the Haas–Lilienthal House is one of the best and most engaging examples remaining in the city. It is now a house museum owned by the San Francisco Architecture Heritage Foundation and remains one of the city's most accessible and well-preserved Queen Anne homes.

The so-called Painted Ladies of San Francisco are, for the most part, not pure Queen Anne houses. The tight groupings of small wooden houses built in San Francisco in the 1880s and 90s retained elements of the Italianate Style, Gothic Revival, and the Stick Style long after their fashion had passed in the East. And although their eclectic exteriors fit right into the expansive attitude toward decoration that characterized the Queen Anne style, they form a regional variation on the theme of a national vernacular architecture.

The Haas–Lilienthal House is named for its longtime occupants, William Haas (1849–1916) and his daughter, Alice Haas Lilienthal (1885–1972). William Haas was born in Bavaria, and like so many others at the time, came to America in his teens to seek his fortune. By 1868, he made his way across the country from New York to San Francisco, and joined a cousin, Kalman Haas, who had already established a grocery business there. Young William's rise in the world was steady. He eventually became president of the firm Haas Brothers, prosperous merchants who supplied the needs of a growing city and its surrounding suburbs. He served as a director of the Wells Fargo Bank, sat on the Board of Arbitration of the San Francisco Chamber of Commerce, and held the position of president of Mt. Zion Hospital for many years. William Haas and his business contacts and friends formed strong bonds of mutual support for the entire Jewish community in San Francisco, but the Bavarians were acknowledged as the leaders, founding and funding most of the city's Jewish charitable and educational organizations.[46]

William Haas, the successful merchant, was married in 1880 at age thirty, to Bertha Greenebaum, the nineteen-year-old daughter of another successful merchant. Her family home was at 1917 Franklin Street, and although people of money and fashion were flocking to Van Ness Avenue one block east, the couple chose to remain on the quieter side street of Franklin as they planned their life together. In 1886, the Haas' purchased land at 2007 Franklin Street, and commissioned a local architect, Peter Schmidt, also a fellow German, to design a house for them.

Schmidt had a long career in San Francisco, beginning with his work as a draftsman in 1863 for the firm of Hoffman & Mooser, and continuing through the nineteenth century when he retired as a partner in his own firm of Schmidt & Shea. Like so many architects of the Queen Anne style, he was not academically trained, but learned on the job, beginning as a draftsman for an established firm, and gradually moving to create his own firm, where he could design his own buildings and oversee their construction. By 1886 Schmidt was a partner in his own firm of Schmidt & Havens, and he was clearly familiar with the vocabulary of the Queen Anne style, with its turrets, porches, gables, and textural effects of different materials. He also had a distinctly local understanding of how to develop the style for the long and narrow lots that characterized San Francisco, and how to use native redwood to best advantage structurally and decoratively.

The house Peter Schmidt designed was for a family, and included twenty-four rooms and seven-and-a-half bathrooms, a kitchen with the latest appliances for the age, and a ballroom or entertaining room in the basement for get-togethers with extended family and friends. The house cost, all told, $18,000, including the purchase of the lot, an astronomical sum for the day. But the money went into quality construction, and careful detailing, so much so that images of the house were published soon after completion in the weekly *San Francisco Newsletter and Advertiser*. In 1888, these serial publications of exemplary houses were collected into a book, *Artistic Homes of California*, containing "Fifty Illustrations of the Handsomest Residences in San Francisco, Oakland and San Jose." The intent of the book was both as a souvenir of a city already hosting thousands of visitors a year, and as a public relations piece to convince people outside of California of "the refinement and elegance of our Homes."[47]

The exterior of the Haas–Lilienthal house reflects the preference for wood that both the style and the climate engendered. Wood is more forgiving of slight structural movements in an earthquake-prone area, and the local redwood was beautiful, extremely durable, and widely available. All the exterior siding, formed into shingles and clapboards, is made of redwood, and the San Francisco Architecture Heritage Foundation, now owner of the house, believes almost all of the present materials to be original to the 1886 construction, a testament to redwood's durability. The first floor of the house has wooden boards laid up in horizontal rows with beveled edges top and bottom, giving the impression of finely cut ashlar masonry. The second floor is largely covered in small, straight shingles, giving a fine-grained texture to the surface. Within the third-floor gables, the shingles are cut with a rounded edge, or fish-scale pattern. Wooden decoration in the cornice, in panels between windows, and under the eaves is carved wood, using stylized foliate motifs. The overall effect is a richness of detail that does not become overwhelming because of the unifying effect of color. The house is painted light gray with white trim, the original colors of the exterior. Although nationally Queen Anne houses were often painted in rich, autumnal hues, San Francisco's foggy atmosphere broken by brilliant sunlight gave rise to a local taste for more subdued hues, such as pale gray, tan, and pale yellow. The animated colors of the San Francisco Painted Ladies are a phenomenon of the 1960s and have no basis in historic color fact.

The foundation and chimneys are red brick; the chimney visible on the south wall was relocated there in an 1898 remodeling. The front entry is sheltered by a porch marked by a pedimented roof and robust turned columns of a fanciful design, while the porch railing is wood imitating a classical stone balustrade. The floor of this entry is made of tiny mosaic tiles, with a beautiful classically patterned border, each laid by hand. San Francisco's mild climate has preserved this detail, which would have been likely lost from houses with more dramatic temperature swings. The paired, antique wood doors with large beveled glass windows inset provided a handsome welcome to the house, and showcased the Haas' wealth and good taste.

The tall, long, and narrow house Schmidt designed for the Haas' largely filled their mid-block lot, 60' wide by 137' deep. Only years later, in 1898, was William Haas able to purchase the lot to the south of

The interior stair hall is flooded with light, both natural and from built-in electric and gas fixtures.

The Haas–Lilienthal House dining room is almost baronial in scale. Native oak woodwork on walls, ceiling, and floors brings color and warmth to the room.

the house in order to create a garden setting for the property. The house is arranged on a traditional town-house plan: entry at one side of the façade leads to a long hall, off of which are arranged rooms, with the most formal (and seldom used) in the front of the house, the family parlor and dining room at the center of the house, and the service areas and kitchen to the rear. What keeps the house from townhouse gloom is that in the progression of rooms from front to back, each steps out with bay windows, bringing light into the house and giving the characteristic irregular outline of the elevation so beloved by the Queen Anne style.

When first built, the interior of the house was focused on a "living hall," where the main staircase was located in a hall space that had a window of colored glass, a fireplace, and a built-in seating area. At least some of these aspects of the living hall, first widely praised in the midcentury revivalists' description of English medieval houses, were widely adopted in American Queen Anne houses, but more as a symbolic gesture to design than a genuinely useful arrangement of space. The Haas' apparently found the space inconvenient, and in 1898, remodeled the first floor and removed the fireplace from the hall and placed a new fireplace into the family parlor. They also removed an "art glass" window on the stair landing, replacing it with clear glass, so as to flood the oak-paneled entry and staircase (which remained from the original design) with daylight.

The description of the interior of the house in the publication *Artistic Homes of California* both documents how well the house has been preserved since 1888, and gives a sense of the colors used in the first period, not all of which are presented in the current interpretation of the house.

> The front parlor, finished in parti-color woodwork, is delicately tinted in light terra-cotta, with cornice in relief in light chocolate. The southeast corner of the room is expanded into the tower windows, giving a grand effect. On the south side is a beautiful mantel of California onyx with a tall mirror [the mirror is no longer present and the onyx fireplace surround is framed by a wooden, columned mantel in the Classical Revival style]. The back parlor, also tinted in terra cotta, is finished in black walnut. The sliding doors between have tall ground glass panels. The dining room is tinted in light olive and finished in antique oak, with dado. The fireplace is set in the west wall, with colored tiles, and crowned by an ornate chimneypiece. [48]

The support spaces for this beautiful house were also of interest to the writer and readers of *Artistic Homes of California*. The description of the interior included a notation of the butler's pantry that opened off the dining room, and mention of the kitchen, laundry, furnace room, storeroom, and wine cellar. [49] Many of these spaces were updated for family use over the century of occupancy, but the updating was more "evolution" than radical change. However, on the second floor, the master bathroom seems to have been hardly touched since 1886, when it represented state-of-the-art indoor plumbing and sanitary facilities. The large, tiled room contains the original tub, showerhead, toilet, bidet, sink, and gas fixtures lighting the mirror above the sink. The beautiful relief-pattern border tile and gracefully molded ceramic forms add elegance to this most utilitarian of rooms.

The master suite at the front of the house included not only this bathroom but also a bedroom and sitting room. Three other bedrooms, a nursery, linen closet, and another bathroom formed the family quarters on the second floor. The third floor provided additional rooms for servants and storage, and as the contemporary description of the house noted, an "unequaled view" of the city and the bay.

TOP: *The original bathroom on the second floor included state-of-the-art technology and sanitary ware: a pedestal sink, a toilet, a bidet, and bathtub with built-in shower, all in a room tiled for easy cleaning.*

BOTTOM: *The kitchen was designed for efficient use for a household that frequently hosted entertainments for dozens, and even hundreds, of people at a time.*

As was characteristic of the Queen Anne style in America, ornate decoration and fanciful design were combined with the latest in technology to provide comfort and ease to inhabitants. The writer for *Artistic Homes of California* concludes the tour of the house by noting "An air of comfort and elegance pervades the house; convenience has been consulted; electricity flies at the command of the slightest touch. The gas fixtures present different effects in bronze, hammered copper, and combinations of oxidized silver and brass."[50]

The combination of gas and electric fixtures was not uncommon in the 1880s, when homebuilders were not entirely sure of the reliability or long-term prospects of electricity, which, as a clean, bright lighting source, was more desirable than gas. A few years later, when electricity was put to use in other household appliances and gadgets, the fate of gas as an obsolete technology was sealed.

William and Bertha Haas raised three children in this house. By the time of the San Francisco earthquake, their eldest daughter had already married and moved to her own home—a few blocks away on Franklin Street! A few years later, in 1909, the youngest Haas daughter, Alice, was married to Samuel Lilienthal in a wedding at her childhood home. This notable social event is said to have had three hundred guests—even in as large a house as this one, it must have been crowded!

Mr. Haas died in 1916. Retired from business, he remained active in philanthropic ventures within the German-Jewish community, and at the time of his death was raising money for relief of German Jews caught up in the horrors of World War I. Their son, Charles, inherited his father's business and continued his family's philanthropic interests. Through marriage, he became related to perhaps the most famous of San Francisco's nineteenth-century German-Jewish mercantile families, the Levi Strausses.

With only widow Bertha in residence in the large old house, Alice and Samuel Lilienthal moved in about 1916. Although she had the wealth to be able to keep up with fashion, Alice Haas-Lilienthal chose to maintain and preserve the Queen Anne–style house largely as it had been during its heyday in her parents' lifetime. She did eventually add a garage to

An upstairs sitting room glows in the light from richly colored stained-glass windows, and from the original gas lighting fixture hanging in the room.

the rear of the garden in 1927, and a new bedroom wing in 1928. Alice Lilienthal lived in the house until her death in 1972, at which time it passed to the San Francisco Architecture Heritage Foundation.

The neighborhood of Victorian-era houses that had once run along this stretch of Franklin Street, populated in no small part by family and friends of the family, and later, Lilienthals, was transformed during the twentieth century into an area of mixed residential high-rises and commercial buildings. The house did survive the 1989 Loma-Prieta earthquake with only minor damage, another testament to the skill of architect Peter Schmidt and the contractors of the 1880s. But once inside this house-museum, the worry of earthquakes and the bustle of modern life fall away against the charm and vivacity of a comfortable Queen Anne–style house. 🏵

BEESON HOUSE, CHICAGO, ILLINOIS

CHICAGO WAS A BOOMTOWN from the moment the fires were put out in 1873. Downtown, new interest in fireproof construction and in maximizing the use of ever-more-valuable lots led to the rapid development of skyscraper building technology in the latter nineteenth century. However, cost and custom soon led to a division between commercial and residential construction for the first time. The downtown skyscrapers and public buildings quickly adopted the new steel-frame technology, and architects sought a new, modern expression for the façades of these most modern of building types. Meanwhile, in many neighborhoods, domestic architecture remained tied to traditional building techniques and appearance, and even reinforced its claim to historical styles. Each man's home was his castle, and each castle proclaimed its solid intention to be around for hundreds of years, its design pedigree stretching hundreds of years back in time.

Although brand new since the 1880s, Chicago's emerging residential neighborhoods often relied on historic styles and solid materials to give the impression of a long-established society. One outstanding house in the city turned the impression of permanence into reality, and the Beeson House is now a designated landmark in the city of Chicago. The Beeson House is a Queen Anne–style house; its coach house is a rare survivor of the outbuildings that accompanied so many historic houses.

Frederick Beeson was the president of the Chicago Veneer Company, a local wood products manufacturing company. He built his home in 1892, to designs by Frederick R. Schock, a local architect. Schock designed several houses in the neighborhood, including his own. The Beeson House is particularly notable for its rusticated limestone base, which extends up into porch walls and supports, giving the house an almost fortresslike foundation. The exaggerated keystones over windows have an Italian Renaissance feel, while the canted columns of stone suggest that the mason was simply frustrated by the inability to get large enough pieces to shape into classical columns.

The upper floors of the house are wooden shingles. In the current dark reddish-orange color, they perfectly suggest the English terra-cotta and tile work that would have been on the Old World examples of Queen Anne architecture. Highlighting the trim work in white paint further reinforces the color effect of the 1880s Queen Anne houses of the Shaw-designed Bedford Park or some other suburban development. The trim work on the Beeson House includes many Classical Revival elements, such as scrollwork pediments over the second-floor windows, and the Palladian window in the front, third-floor gable.

Asymmetrical arrangement of the massing and the totally functional placement of windows within the elevations produce the irregular charm, or "picturesque" quality that was a valued aesthetic judgment at the end of the nineteenth century. The Beeson House has the corner tower, under a shallow conical roof, arranged next to the gable-front façade, creating a typical composition for the Queen Anne style. But more than usual, this house has a strong central axis under the projecting front gable, including the large front windows directly aligned on both upper floors, and the main entrance underneath. Thus both the design and materials combine to create a Queen Anne house of particular gravity and permanence, in marked contrast to some of the lighter and more whimsical examples of the style.

The coach house to the rear of the property has a high first floor with a single garage door, and a low second floor inserted under the eaves of the pyramidal roof. The Gothic arch of the dormer and the projecting bay window at the first floor introduce architectural elements different from those found on the

Spectacular leaded glass, Roman brick fireplace, and the staircase that turns back on itself are all hallmarks of this sophisticated Queen Anne living hall.

OPPOSITE: *The main staircase incorporates large landings at each level and in-between.*

main house. The overall effect of the coach house is of a small cottage, in harmony with, although not matching the main house.

Inside the Beeson House, one enters a real Queen Anne living hall, with the main staircase at one side of a large comfortable room. The fireplace is within a broad wall of terra-cotta–colored Roman brick, and the fireplace flue is cleverly angled to place a stained-glass window directly above the hearth. Thus, when it is daylight, golden light comes from above; when it is dark and the fire lit, the golden light comes from below. The coloristic effects continue with the dark brown of the oak-paneled staircase, which is burnished by the golden light coming through the gold- and green-colored glass in the tiny-paned windows in the stair.

Patterned wallpapers on walls and ceiling illustrate the pinnacle of interior decorating in the Queen Anne style.

Opening off this center space are the other rooms of the house, each flooded with natural light through the large single-pane windows. The dining-room fireplace has a broad mantel tiled in gold-and-green hued art tiles laid in an abstract pattern. The warm reddish-brown of the cherry woodwork in this room provides a color complement.

In all the main rooms, the plaster ceiling rises up in coved corners over a picture rail. The wooden picture rail was placed in many homes in the Victorian era to allow for easy changes to the pictures and mirrors hanging on the walls, and to prevent damage to the wallpaper.

Period fixtures remind us that the Queen Anne house was the first architecture reliably lighted by electricity. The period bathroom in the house recalls the Queen Anne interest in sanitation and plumbing. Despite the outward trappings of historical style, the Queen Anne house was thoroughly modern in its technology and function.

The patterned tile used on the fireplace is set off by the dark wood wainscot that surrounds the room.

The neighborhood of the Beeson House was laid out in 1865 by Henry Austin, and was planned to include public water and sewers; later, the local council encouraged the early introduction of electricity to the community. Created as a solidly middle-class suburban enclave, the area had swift and reliable transportation to Chicago's downtown Loop, just seven-and-a-half miles to the east. The enclave was known as the village of Austin until annexed by the city of Chicago in 1899; it remains the most populous individual neighborhood recognized within the borders of the City of Chicago. Austin was known in the latter nineteenth century for Queen Anne–style architecture by its local architect Frederick Schock. Historical styles including Colonial Revival, Tudor Revival, and Mediterranean Revival continued to be built along the streets of Austin well into the twentieth century. The Beeson House remains a private home, but a walk along the streets of the Austin neighborhood reveals that it is one of many fine examples of the Queen Anne style in the area. 🌸

The juxtaposition of delicately carved decoration and the solid mass of the walls is part of the charm of the Queen Anne style.

OPPOSITE: *The carriage house is located behind the main house across a lovely garden.*

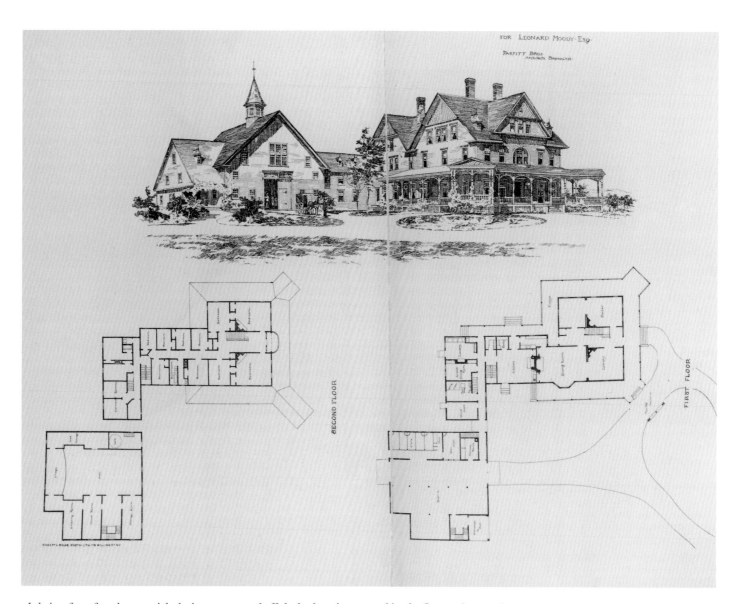

A design for a farmhouse, with the barn connected off the back, as interpreted in the Queen Anne style.

RURAL HOUSES

RURAL COMMUNITIES WERE JUST as interested as their city cousins in the latest developments in technology, home-building, and architectural style. The Queen Anne style came to the attention of farm families and their builders though farm magazines or other periodicals, which typically published house plans and interior decorating information in the nineteenth century. *The American Agriculturalist* was the largest-circulation periodical in America in the nineteenth century. Its pages were filled with things the progressive, prosperous farmer wanted to know: information on new breeds of hogs, the latest in farm equipment, and how to increase yields of corn. But it also included designs for barns, stables, and houses, and the magazine even occasionally included information on interior decorating, formal table setting, flower arranging, and other things that enhanced the beauty of life in the country.

Rural houses are particularly interesting in that they are most likely to retain tried-and-true elements at their functional heart, and graft onto the building only the minimum of ornament or detailing to make the house look as though it shares in the popular taste. This is clearly seen when the highly decorative Queen Anne style was incorporated into rural dwellings.

During the years when the Queen Anne style was popular in the United States, the country passed a significant demographic milestone. In 1893, history professor Frederick Jackson Turner published his famous thesis, claiming "The frontier has gone, and with its going has closed the first period of American history." The United States Census of 1890 had determined that there was no longer a demarcation between the "settled" and the "empty" places within the United States, and all development from that moment on was "filling in" the existing country rather than continuously expanding into a new, unknown land. Although it is not filled up yet, today the majority of Americans live in urban places.

In the 1890s, however, the majority of Americans still lived in rural places—not frontier, but either in very small, distinct towns or on individual farmsteads, and this would continue to be the case for several more decades. The three houses in this section illustrate the influence of the Queen Anne style in rural places in America. John Lindale built a house in the crossroads settlement of Magnolia, Delaware, to proclaim his wealth earned from peach orchards, which once spread as far as the eye could see around his home. The Krabbenhoft Farmhouse is the centerpiece of a northern plains wheat farm, established by German immigrants who homesteaded to earn their land. The Ovide Broussard House shows the merger of the distinctive regional architecture of the Cajuns with the Queen Anne style as the representative of modernity and progress in a small town made rich by the commercial cultivation of rice.

JOHN LINDALE HOUSE, MAGNOLIA, DELAWARE

THE FLAT, SANDY DELMARVA Peninsula includes the state of Delaware and parts of Maryland and Virginia. The land has been intensively used for agriculture for hundreds of years, although the crops produced have varied over time. In the second half of the nineteenth century, peach trees were the most common sight on farms in Delaware. Fresh peaches were shipped by train to urban markets, and were priced as a luxury item because ripe peaches required careful handling at every step between picker and consumer to avoid bruised fruit. Much of the fruit was cooked and put into tin cans, and then shipped to markets year-round. The peach industry peaked in the 1890s, when, by one estimate, five million peach trees stood in Delaware, yielding a crop worth thousands and thousands of dollars. In their honor, the Delaware state legislature named the peach blossom the state flower in May 1895.

One of the biggest and most successful peach growers in central Delaware in the 1880s and 90s was John Lindale (1864–1937). He successfully bought up many small farms and modernized them, according to the most progressive precepts of the time, by turning to large, commercial-scale agriculture and forsaking the old-fashioned model of diversified family farms. John Lindale saw the future of agriculture as a business, and himself as not just a "farmer." In the 1900 U.S. Census, he alone in his community of farmers and laborers is listed as "Capitalist"[51] An ambitious young man, he married in 1886, and proceeded to have a house built for himself and his bride which expressed his wealth and standing in the community.

He erected a Queen Anne–style house in the village of Magnolia, to this day, a village of just over 250 people. It was the biggest house in town, and the most startlingly up-to-date in a community that until then boasted only the simplest frame houses of local vernacular style. The house is punctuated by two tall towers and a roof-top balcony, where he could have seen far across the flat landscape to his farms all around the village.

The love of pattern and texture so characteristic of the Queen Anne style is evident in the slate roof, with diamond-pattern and square-cut shingles alternating in bands. The wooden siding repeats the theme, with clapboard siding contrasting with wooden shingles and diagonally laid tongue-and-groove boarding in the panels under the windows of the towers. There is no masonry of note on the building—the brick foundation and chimney are simple, utilitarian affairs—unlike more sophisticated examples of the style. However, the bold projecting front gable with a round arched window in it, the heavily dentiled cornice, and the fluted columns supporting the deep porch are strongly progressive elements of the Queen Anne style, with overtones of the classicism the underpins the style, at least in its English beginnings.

Inside the house, the front door leads to a stair hall, with the stairs rising gracefully to an oval balcony. The turned spindles of the stair and the chunky newel post, with the original clear finish on wood, are very characteristic of the Queen Anne style. The library mantel is, if anything, old-fashioned for the 1880s with its knobs and geometric designs. Another mantel in the parlor is more modern and returns to the early Colonial Revival influence that may sometimes be seen in Queen Anne buildings, through the swag motif applied to it. Interior wooden shutters throughout the house are original, and typical of a popular device for controlling light in Queen Anne interiors. Though the big house may have been built in anticipation of a large family, John and Eliza Lindale never had any children.

OPPOSITE: *Two turrets and a rooftop observation deck originally afforded a view across the small town of Magnolia and the flat rural landscape to the peach orchards that provided John Lindale with the means to build this fashionable house.*

There are several outbuildings on the property, including the small out-kitchen placed immediately to the rear of the Lindale House.

The sitting room has a boldly designed mantel in wood, the country substitute for elaborate tiled examples found in more urbanized houses.

OPPOSITE: *The oval window echoes the oval turn in the landing on the second floor.*

Lindale's builder was Charles G. Fisher, of Milford, Delaware, the nearest town of any consequence. Fisher was, like many of the perpetrators of the Queen Anne style in America, not a trained architect, although in the 1900 Census he is identified in occupation as a "civil engineer." The label "architect" or "engineer" could still be earned through apprenticeship at this time. Any formal training Fisher may have had in the building arts is unknown. But it is clear that he was aware of popular styles, like the Queen Anne, and he executed a fine example for the Lindales.

The John Lindale property is notable for its excellent state of preservation, attributable in large part to the fact that Eliza lived there until her death in 1961, and subsequent owners saw themselves very clearly as custodians of many original features and furnishings inside

Slatted window shutters were an original window treatment in the late nineteenth century.

and outside the house that had survived for so long already. The other reason for its remarkable preservation may be attributed to the "peach blight," which began to attack trees in the 1890s. By 1900, most of the trees in Delaware had been cut down and burned in an effort to thwart the virus, and John Lindale's fortune went up in smoke with them. The blight hit orchards all over the East Coast, but perhaps nowhere was it felt as sharply as in Delaware, which had established a nearly monolithic agricultural economy in peaches. While Lindale and other farmers struggled to find a new cash crop, there were no alterations to the old house.

The in-town complex of house, garden, barn, sheds, and a wire fence enclosing the yard is a remarkable slice of small-town America from about 1900, preserved in the twenty-first century. 🏵

TOP: *Decorative designs enriched even mundane things in the latter nineteenth century.*

BOTTOM: *Wooden shingles, cut to a fish-scale shape were particularly popular.*

KRABBENHOFT FARMHOUSE, SABIN, MINNESOTA

THE NEWS FROM SABIN, Minnesota, at least as published in the local *Moorhead Independent* newspaper for 1901, included at least two notes on the construction of Fred Krabbenhoft's house, and both reported that it would be "one of the finest residences in Clay County."[52] Nestled in a wooded bend near the South Buffalo River, the Krabbenhoft Farm is today on the National Register of Historic Places, notable for its association with pioneer settlers of the area and the remarkable house they built.

Wolf Krabbenhoft (with an American nickname of "Fred"), was born in Germany in 1845. From the time of his birth, the various German states, including Schleswig-Holstein, where the Krabbenhofts lived, were at war with each other, and with neighboring Denmark and Austria. Several men of the family had already been conscripted into the army, some had perished on the battlefield, and young Wolf was uninterested in taking up the soldier's life. So he emigrated to the United States at age nineteen, steps ahead of the German leader Bismark's newly inaugurated Prussian Military Service Law. He went first to Iowa, then to California, and then in 1872, took up a homestead in Minnesota.

The United States Homestead Act of 1862, signed into law by Abraham Lincoln, turned over vast amounts of the public domain to private citizens. Almost 10 percent of the land area of the United States, or 270 million acres, was claimed and settled under this act. A homesteader had only to be the head of a household and at least twenty-one years of age to claim a 160-acre parcel of land. Settlers from all walks of life including newly arrived immigrants, farmers without land of their own from the East, single women, and former slaves came to meet the challenge of "proving up" and keeping this "free land." Homesteaders had to live on the land, build a home, make improvements and farm for five years in order to prove, by neighbor's affidavits, that they had indeed created a homestead on the land. A total filing fee of eighteen dollars was the only money required, but sacrifice and hard work exacted a different price from the hopeful settlers.

As a homesteader, Fred agreed to build a house and begin farming in order to keep the claim on 160 acres of land. His brother, Christopher, who also emigrated from Germany, joined him in getting to work and establishing the farm. Over the next several years, the rest of their family arrived in the United States, including Wolf and Christopher's parents. It was hard work, but their steady successes brought other German immigrants to the valley, and soon there were neighbors, and then marriages, and then children and a rural community was established with its local nexus in Moorhead, a village about seven miles away. The original home for Fred and Christopher was described as a "dugout" along the riverbank, then he and Christopher had a wooden "shanty"; as more people joined them, other housing was constructed, with varying degrees of sophistication.

A new wooden house went up on the property in 1878, when Fred Krabbenhoft married Marie Jensen, also an immigrant to America. In 1882, the Wolf "Fred" Krabbenhoft Homestead claim was "proved" and he was granted title to the farm. He eventually owned 1,800 acres of prime land in Clay County. The couple and their farm endured good times and bad, but the good generally overcame the bad. They had thirteen children together; nine lived to adulthood. Marie's widowed father joined their household upon his wife's death. In order to work the farm, the Krabbenhofts had two live-in helpers, one a member of their extended family who acted as a general farm laborer, and John Brenner, a German-born carpenter. With so many in the household by 1900, Fred and Marie planned a new house for themselves. In thrifty farm fashion, however, their old house was moved to another farm and remodeled for another family's use.

Woodwork with incised sides and "bulls-eye" corner blocks.

The new Krabbenhoft House was built in 1901, relying on a basic rectangular plan and the five-bay, center-entry form that has been part of America's vernacular landscape since the eighteenth century. The house was covered with wooden shingles, which reflect the sensibilities of the Queen Anne style. A simple projecting gable extends from the main block of the house to create a sheltered entry porch on the first floor and a prominent location for a decorative Palladian window in the attic. Lacy wooden trim in the projecting gable and at the porch provide the sum of the decoration on the otherwise straightforward house, but it is enough to clearly identify that the house was influenced by the Queen Anne style, and no other. The roof ridge is surmounted by lacy iron cresting, a detail often found on nineteenth-century houses to give added "picturesque" details to the top of the house.

To create their dream house, the Krabbenhofts did not hire an architect. Like many other people, they hired local carpenters, and simply told them what they wanted. The builders relied on their experience, rather than drawn plans, to provide the basic structure, and thus it reflects a long-standing building tradition of what worked best for the climate and materials available. Any decorative touches were strictly add-ons to the basic building.

The Queen Anne style came to the attention of the Krabbenhofts and their builders, probably though farm magazines or other periodicals, which typically published house plans and interior decorating information in the nineteenth century. While suburban houses took up the bulk of the design space in period-

The Krabbenhoft Farm includes the grain elevator, built in 1911.

icals and pattern books, many sources recognized that there was in America in the 1880s and 90s still a large rural population, and the farm family was just as interested in keeping their home up-to-date as the suburban or urban dweller. A publication of 1878 specifically showed how to remodel older houses into "modern" ones in the Stick Style or Queen Anne style. The results were often awkward, but that hardly deterred people from trying. No less a source than *Architecture and Building*, a periodical aimed at the architects and builders of America, published a design in 1891 of a farmhouse in Maine, and remodeled to reflect the latest fashions. A standard feature all of these remodelings was the addition of a projecting center gable, like the one on the Krabbenhoft house.

The interior of the Krabbenhoft House reflects the same straightforward attitude toward design as the farm itself—neat, functional, and with just enough detail to keep it visually interesting. The wooden wainscot in the lower part of the dining-room walls, and the pressed metal ceiling added the texture demanded in the Queen Anne interior, while providing more sturdy and easy-to-clean surfaces than tapestries and wallpapers. The projecting bay over the front entry provides a sunny seating area at the end of the second-floor hall. Although probably not used much by a busy farm family, it offered at least the promise of leisure.

The Krabbenhofts invested in fancy hardware, including the floral-rimmed bronze pulls that still remain on the pocket doors between front and back parlors. The interior was professionally painted, and wallpapers (no longer extant) were hung. In a period family photograph, presumably taken in this house, a young woman sits at an upright piano. Behind her, the dark tones of a floral wallpaper rise, and a picture rail divides that pattern from another dark border pattern. Before hanging the paper, however, a craftsman drew two pencil sketches of Fred and Marie directly on the plaster wall. They are informal, closely observed portraits. An old man, with a wrinkled forehead, bald head, and a long full beard sits in a chair "resting his eyes." A dumpling of a woman, with curly hair escaping her bun, is shown in profile. These sketches and, elsewhere on the plaster wall the names "L. Peterson" and "L. Johnson" inscribed with a flourish, were later found.

A check of the U.S. Census records of 1900 finds Louis Johnson, Norwegian by birth and a painter by profession, living nearby in Elmwood Township, Clay County. Johnson and Peterson must have

worked in the Krabbenhoft's House on the finishes, affectionately recording their clients in a private moment before continuing their work. Later homeowners, stripping wallpaper, found the pencil sketches, and have preserved them and made them visible by applying a frame over them directly onto the wall.

For Fred, the house was the fulfillment of his American dream, the culmination of all he had worked for, starting with those first hard years of breaking the sod, while living in a cave. He lived until 1910, and then died in his new home following a fall from a wagon, presumed to have been caused by a stroke.

TOP LEFT AND RIGHT: *Fred and Marie Krabbenhoft, as sketched on the walls of their house in 1900.*

BOTTOM: *Early twentieth-century photo of the house.*

The farmstead's other important buildings—the horse barn (1890), the cow barn (1900), the machine shed (1905), and the grain elevator (1911) reflect the pride of a family intent on running a neat and profitable farm. Fred Krabbenhoft, and his successor on the property, his youngest son Otto (1890–1981), maintained traditional—and sustainable—farming practices long after others turned to more machine-intensive practices. They used horses to pull the plow long after neighboring farmers adopted tractors; when the Krabbenhofts finally went to tractors, they used small ones, and shunned the ever-larger equipment that made its way onto farms. The Krabbenhofts, father and son, farmed here for ninety years; now another family maintains the farm and its charming buildings are well preserved.

The current owners of the house deserve all praise and credit for generously sharing so much material about the Krabbenhoft family, including photographs, original newspaper articles, and the book, *Krabbenhofts and Kin 1872–1949,* by Elsa Krabbenhoft Radichel.

OVIDE BROUSSARD HOUSE, ABBEVILLE, LOUISIANA

THE CANADIAN PROVINCE OF ACADIA (today's Nova Scotia and surrounding regions) was settled in the early 1700s by French colonists, but the area became a British possession soon afterward. In 1755, as war neared between France and England, the British authorities demanded that the Acadians renounce their Roman Catholic faith and swear allegiance to the Crown. The Acadians refused, choosing mass exile over conformity; the exodus that followed was immortalized in the poem "Evangeline" by Henry Wadsworth Longfellow. The Acadian people scattered across North America, and some went back to France, but a large group eventually made their way to coastal Louisiana, part of France's colonial empire. Here they established small farms along the Mississippi River, Bayou Teche, Bayou Lafourche, and other streams. The Cajun (the word is a corruption of the original French pronunciation of Acadian: A-ca-jan) people came to be focused in the swampy lowlands of Louisiana west of New Orleans, where they hunted and trapped; the land being unsuitable for anything like traditional agriculture that the Acadians had known.

Adapting to a warmer, wetter climate than either France or Nova Scotia, the Cajuns developed their own regional culture, with its own foods, language, music, and architecture. Even after the Louisiana Purchase of 1803 made the Louisiana Territory part of the United States, the Cajuns continued their distinctive traditions. These were nurtured and preserved for many decades by the geographic isolation of their communities and their economy, which did not require much connection to the larger world. But with the coming of the railroad in the latter nineteenth century, these communities were knitted into the larger American whole. Opportunities for growth, and for interaction, increased, and the Cajuns began to adopt American ideas, integrating them with their traditional and regional ways.

The little town of Abbeville, on the Vermillion River, lies within "Cajun Country." It was founded in 1843 as the location for a Catholic chapel in a rural region; by 1854 it became the parish seat of newly created Vermillion Parish. It was not until 1892, with the opening of the Iberia and Vermillion Railroad (soon to be incorporated into the Southern Pacific Railroad) that the town experienced any significant growth.

With ready access to national markets through the railroad, the farmers in and around Abbeville, as well as in other low-lying Louisiana towns, were able to take advantage of the mechanized agricultural techniques that had opened the Great Plains to commercial farming. But instead of wheat, it was rice that thrived in this climate, and it was the "Great Louisiana Rice Boom" of the years 1895 to 1910 that introduced the Queen Anne style of architecture to the small town of Abbeville.

Abbeville's population more than doubled during the rice boom, from 1,200 souls in 1895 to over 2,500 in 1907. Abbeville has a distinctive collection of houses from the turn of the last century that reflects the merger of traditional Cajun single-story housing types with the nationally popular Queen Anne style. These houses give a physical form to the new wealth and sophistication that came to the region at the end of the nineteenth century because of the commercial agricultural production of rice for a national market.

Rice farmers themselves were perhaps the last to profit from the rice boom. The railroads that shipped the grain; the sellers of farm equipment and fertilizer; and the bankers that backed the expansion

The traditional house type of the Cajuns was a single-story frame dwelling with a high hipped roof which extended to form porches around the building.

A projecting gable over a bay window and decorative porch trim transform a traditional Cajun vernacular house to a practical variation of the Queen Anne style.

into new land and new equipment saw bigger profits sooner than those who labored in the rice paddies. In the town of Abbeville, an enterprising young man named Ovide Broussard went to work for the local bank and through the good luck of coming of age along with the rice boom, soon made his fortune.

The Broussards were one of the old Cajun families, and there was at least one other Ovide Broussard living in that small town in the 1890s as well as others of that name in the region. This particular Ovide Broussard had married, by the age of twenty-two, a local girl named Paula Brasseux. The 1900 Census noted that Ovide's occupation was "Assistant Cashier Bank" making him one of a small cadre of "professionals" in Abbeville at that period. As Abbeville prospered, the bank did too, and with it Ovide Broussard. Thirty years later, Ovide Broussard was vice-president of the bank and had amassed a substantial personal net worth. [53]

When Ovide Broussard and his wife had their second child in 1899 (a son, named Ovide, naturally) they needed a new house. The young couple stretched to build their dream house, and for some time, Adolph Brasseux—Paula's brother, a salesman—lived with them, his income helping to support the household. The three adults eventually were surrounded by Ovide and Paula's six children.

The Broussard's new house was a cottage reflecting the fashionable Queen Anne style, but one that grafted these modern details onto a much older, and very familiar form in the region. Ovide Broussard's

High ceilings and a hall with doors at either end help to keep the house cool during the summers.

house, built about 1899, is one of the best examples of a hybrid style of Queen Anne architecture and traditional Cajun dwellings. The basic form of the house is of a single-story cottage set under a high hipped roof. This is a traditional French architectural form, with roots in medieval times, and adapted to the New World through its execution in wood and the addition of porches. Examples remain throughout the French-settled regions of North America, including in Nova Scotia, Louisiana, and up the Mississippi River to the areas first explored and settled in the eighteenth century by the French.

At Ovide Broussard's house, a central bay was added to this basic form to project out from the façade, creating a focal point for the decorative woodwork of the Queen Anne style. On traditional Cajun houses, the porch or "gallerie" would run across the entire façade; here the projection of the front bay creates two separate porches. One porch leads to the house's main entry, the other porch, which cannot be reached from the exterior of the house, creates a private retreat off a bedroom.

The main entrance to the Ovide Broussard House is a traditional double door with sidelights and transom lights framing it, an entry arrangement that may be found on high-style houses in Louisiana throughout the nineteenth century. The survival of this form attests to the strong hold of tradition in a community like Abbeville, and also the perfect utility of a design that allows plenty of light into the main hall.

Instead of opening into a Queen Anne living hall, the Broussard House retains a traditional floor plan as well, with a front and back door to the entrance hall allowing breezes to flow through. Off to one side is a parlor, on the other side of the hall lies the dining room. Both have half-walls with columns in the upper portion, allowing the distinction of rooms to remain while permitting as much air circulation as possible throughout the house. The high ceiling height is another adaptation to the climate found in traditional Cajun houses, which also worked well with the Queen Anne style. Tall windows let in light and breezes; the surrounding woodwork has the incised, stylized patterns of the Eastlake-inspired interior. The main-floor bedroom opens directly onto the porch on the other side of the front-facing bay window.

Although many Queen Anne–style houses are often accented by towers or turrets, the Louisiana Queen Anne house relies on the generally horizontal form of its traditional predecessor, the Cajun house. There are examples of this hybrid type around the state that incorporate slender turrets, but the Ovide Broussard House is more typical of Louisiana interpretations of the Queen Anne style because of the absence of a tower. Yet the Broussard House and many more like it are undeniably Queen Anne. The projecting front gable extends over a bay window, and in the pediment of the gable, a diamond pattern in wood recalls, ever so faintly, the half-timbering of the original English models for the style. The spindle-work frieze on the porch on the exterior is a decorative nod to the banded friezes of Eastlake interiors, and can be found on Queen Anne houses across America.

Hinges (TOP) *and push plates* (BOTTOM) *give rich detail to the Queen Anne cottage.*

OPPOSITE: *Half walls open up the floor plan of the Queen Anne house.*

High ceilings and tall windows reflect regional building traditions to accommodate the hot climate.

Today, the Ovide Broussard House is privately owned and well maintained, part of a large historic district within Abbeville. The legacy of the "Rice Boom" is written in the concentration of Queen Anne houses from the 1890s and early twentieth century in Abbeville; the corresponding collapse of the local economy when agricultural production declined may be read in the absence of later houses and later styles. The Queen Anne style's great popularity across America was in its intrinsic eclecticism, which allowed clients and builders to graft new decorations onto older and more familiar forms. The Queen Anne style encouraged individuality and discouraged strict adherence to rules for what a building "should" look like. That attitude distressed the trained architects of the day who believed there were steadfast rules for producing beautiful buildings. But the charming results of Queen Anne's introduction to American vernacular building are evident in places like the Ovide Broussard House, where the best of traditional building is successfully merged with new ideas in design.

Paired front doors with windows in them, surrounded by a transom and sidelights,
provide plenty of light into the center hall of the Broussard House.

HOUSES IN TOWN

THE AMERICAN QUEEN ANNE STYLE is, in a way, the visual expression of a John Philip Sousa march. Both were popular, showy, and discounted by the serious critics of the day. Sousa was composing and conducting in the 1880s and 90s, at the very moment the Queen Anne style was working its way into American architecture across the country. Sousa and his band played in cities, but also traveled to smaller towns all across America. He was a genuine "superstar," a popular music phenomenon. The image of the brass band, performing Sousa on a summer's evening at a gazebo in the heart of a small town, is an inescapable image in America's own perception of itself at the turn of the last century.

Look around that park. Ringing it are wooden houses, many in the Queen Anne style. They make up the neighborhoods that are still vital in many towns. Located only a few blocks from the commercial downtown, the Queen Anne houses were set within small lots, and connected by a high canopy of street trees. Located within easy walking distance of a train station, or a park, and always graced with a porch that allows residents to sit and watch the passersby of an evening, these late nineteenth-century neighborhoods are the original form of the pedestrian-friendly development pattern known as "New Urbanism." The Queen Anne neighborhood is found in large and small towns, and provides one of the most quintessentially "American" environments.

Houses in towns across America are highlighted in this chapter. Some are custom-creations of a local architect, like the Milton Carson House in Eureka, California, or the Shelton–McMurphey House in Eugene, Oregon. Others, like the Piatt House in Tunkhannock, Pennsylvania, were created from a mass-produced plan, sold through a book, and mail-ordered by a homeowner located far from the designer. The Elisa Michael House in Galveston, Texas, and the John Fahnestock House in Galesburg, Illinois, both reflect the incorporation of pattern book ideas into the repertoire of a now-anonymous local builder.

In all these places, the Queen Anne houses were built by individuals who were actively involved with their communities over their lifetimes. Their new, fashionable houses reflected personal success, and their pride in doing their own part to improve the appearance of their town. These houses are not part of a larger development controlled by a single builder or suburb designer. Looking at them on a summer evening in the gathering twilight, one hears Sousa marches, playing softly in the distance.

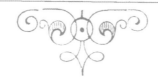

JOHN FAHNESTOCK HOUSE, GALESBURG, ILLINOIS

THROUGHOUT THE SECOND HALF of the nineteenth century, the hissing and chugging of steam locomotives could be heard across America. Trains helped distribute the agricultural wealth and industrial products of the United States all across the land, and prompted the settlement of ever-more western regions of the country. The sound of steam locomotives was particularly clear in the town of Galesburg, Illinois. Like many other towns across America, its development and growth was directly affected by the construction of a railroad, the Chicago, Burlington & Quincy Railroad, which arrived in 1854. But the small town received a big boost after the Civil War when the Atchison, Topeka & Santa Fe Railroad was persuaded to extend its line from the Mississippi to Chicago, and to lay a route through Galesburg. The presence of two railroad lines and their associated business activities in this town proved strong enough in 1873 to have the county seat relocated to Galesburg, from Knoxville, Illinois.

The late nineteenth century saw a construction boom in town, creating a modern business district, and neighborhoods that reflected the community's prosperity. The town had been laid out on the prototypical mid-Western grid plan in 1837, creating straight streets enclosing undifferentiated blocks. But the railroad tracks of the Atchison, Topeka & Santa Fe Railroad, and of the Burlington Northern, cut sharp diagonals across the tidy grid of the town, giving hierarchy to the neighborhoods, with those well away from the railroad sidings and warehouses becoming the preferred locations in town.

Away from the rail tracks, but never out of hearing range of the whistle from a locomotive, North Prairie Street developed as the neighborhood where most of the town's elite lived in the last quarter of the nineteenth century. Houses were built to telegraph their owner's importance, their wealth, and their "good taste." Because the upsurge in Galesburg's economic good fortune came in the 1880s and 90s, many of the most impressive houses are in the Queen Anne style. The original owners were local lawyers, merchants, and above all, railroad men,

One of these men was John C. Fahnestock (1839–1929), a prominent local merchant, a book seller in his early years, who relied on the railroad to bring books, paper, and periodicals from port cities to stock his store. Later, he turned to the railroad for employment, and he became an agent for the Atchison, Topeka & Santa Fe Railroad, helping them to acquire land for new tracks, stations, and investment purposes. As John Fahnestock rose in the world, he began to imagine a fine new house for himself and his family, and the dream was finally realized in 1890 with the construction of his house on North Prairie Avenue.

Fahnestock and his family—his wife, Grace, and daughters Fannie and Grace Amelia—moved into a house that included the most popular elements of American Queen Anne style. The designer, who is unknown, was certainly a local carpenter-builder who took his design inspiration from pattern books, magazines, or other published materials that reached Galesburg by railroad. The house is large and nearly square in plan, set under a high front-facing gable roof, but the designer-builder managed to break up the mass of the house by introducing a rounded tower on the corner, projecting bay windows on each side, and semicircular shapes used as a decorative motif in several places.

Much of the decoration is focused on the two publicly visible sides of the house, as it occupies a prominent corner lot. The rear elevation is plain clapboard with simple windows; functional but unremarkable in design. Similar treatments on houses across the country led to the quip that such buildings had a "Queen Anne front and a Mary Ann behind." The surface texture of the Fahnestock House is derived from clapboard and fish-scale shingles, vertically laid flushboard in the tower cornice and in the tops of gables, and a gridlike lattice pattern.

Entry to the house is gained from the broad porch, built up on a base of rusticated, local sandstone and incorporating stone stairs. This adaptation to native building materials and traditions is indicative of the Queen Anne style; in an area without a good local building stone, the base of a similar house might be raised on brick piers with wooden latticework between them. The stone base on the Fahnestock House made for a durable foundation and stairs, and anchors the house to the ground. Above the stone, the more delicate porch woodwork, including slender columns, latticework, and turned spindles, provides the light decorative touch that is more commonly associated with the style.

At the top of the steps, double doors of beautifully figured wood mark the main entrance to the house. It is unusual that these doors do not incorporate a window, as was increasingly popular toward the end of the nineteenth century, but the carving, with sunburst motifs, is well done, and the motif is repeated on panels elsewhere on the house.

The interior of the Fahnestock House is well illuminated by natural light, so the absence of glass panes in the front doors does not cast the hall into darkness. On the main floor, the staircase, with multiple landings and a paneled and turned balustrade, echoes the design first expressed in the Watts Sherman House. The staircase in the classic Queen Anne house is treated like a room within a room, one that both obscures and reveals its nature. Here, the bottom steps spill out into a larger entrance-living hall, while the screen of the lower baluster obscures the next run of the staircase. The staircase and hall receive ample natural light from tall windows, which have brilliantly colored glass set in the transom above the operable, clear pane.

A room now used as the dining room includes a fireplace, accented with an oak mantel and art-tile surround. "Art tiles" were the rage in the 1880s and 90s in the United States and England. Manufacturers were experimenting with different colors of glaze, and mottled and subtly multicolored glazes were very popular. Tiles were created with low relief designs, depicting mythological figures and stories, scenes from nature, and more stylized motifs, such as swags and frets. At the Fahnestock House, the dining room art tiles depict birds, with flying birds in front of a rising sun as the central motif at the top. The fireplace opening is filled in with a non-opening, decoratively patterned cast-iron panel. It was not at all unusual during the Queen Anne period to see great decorative care lavished on a completely nonfunctional fireplace. It retained great symbolic significance to the Victorian homeowner, but the house was actually warmed through a basement furnace connecting through steam pipes to the big cast iron radiators in all the principal rooms.

However, there were still drafts, and the wide openings between rooms in a typical Queen Anne plan could leave inhabitants longing for the comforts of a fire in the hearth. Instead, proper homes of the era often use portieres, or drapes hung between rooms, to provide for winter draft control. They also contributed to the rich coloration and decoration of the interior, providing yet another opportunity for the display of material abundance that was so beloved by the late nineteenth-century homemaker. The recreation of the use of portieres in the Fahnestock House is a period detail that adds to the sense of its interior's authenticity.

Throughout the first floor of the Fahnestock House, the wooden trim work is clear-finished, another authentic touch, as this was the appropriate treatment for the period. With the rise in popularity of the Colonial Revival in the twentieth century, taste changed from natural wood to painted woodwork. There

Portieres, or heavy drapes, were popular in the Queen Anne period.

are countless Queen Anne houses that have had their woodwork—often oak, or pine stained to a dark "mahogany" tone—overpainted in white or ivory. It is so common today that we don't realize how odd that would have looked to the Queen Anne designers and residents, who celebrated the use of wood and wanted to see its grain and hue. The newly mass-produced varnishes made this possible. Like so many things in the Queen Anne interior, a varnish or clear finish in the preindustrial era was extremely expensive to produce, and generally reserved for fine furniture, not for architectural use. So its appearance as a mass-production item made it available for use in ways that had not been possible before, including for interior architectural finishes. It was this sort of innovative use of a newly available industrially-produced material to reproduce historical designs that proved so desirable to the supporters of the Queen Anne style.

Today the John Fahnestock House is a popular bed and breakfast, which allows people to live, if only temporarily, in the Queen Anne style. It is located in the Galesburg Historic District, which covers more than one thousand buildings, most of them residential, which showcase the architectural styles of the late nineteenth century. The historic district includes "Old Main," an 1851 Knox College building that is the only remaining structure to have hosted one of the famous Lincoln-Douglas debates.

The historic district gives the Fahnestock House and its neighbors the appropriate setting in which to appreciate their architecture. John Fahnestock's neighbor, George Lawrence, an attorney in Galesburg, also had a Queen Anne–style house constructed for himself and his family. Built a year after Fahnestock's, the Lawrence House was all stone, and at $80,000, proved to be the most expensive house constructed in Galesburg in the nineteenth century. Did John Fahnestock feel some envy when he looked out to see the enormous stone house of his neighbor? Or pride that the little town of Galesburg could boast so many beautiful, modern houses?

Around the corner, on North Broad Street, three Queen Anne–style houses stand in a row, each one presenting variations of the theme of the style as constructed in wood. All were constructed in 1894; local lore suggests that the plans for these houses were on display at the Chicago World Columbia Exposition held in 1893, and that local druggist and store owner Will Lescher decided to have the houses reproduced in Galesburg. He moved into one; his friend and colleague, Dr. Luster, who had his offices above the Lescher Drug Company downtown, moved into another; and a third, built on speculation, provided rents to cover the entrepreneurs' costs. All three originally had porte cocheres and were said to have had ballrooms in the third floor. The middle house, built for rental purposes, includes a tower, and round-arched windows and porte-cochere opening that echo the use of the form in the Fahnestock House. Its tall corner turret, half-timbered gable, and tall, steep roofs, all in wood, are so removed from the architecture of the seventeenth century Queen Anne that she could not possibly have recognized it. They are even quite different from the English architecture of the 1870s and 80s that gave the name "Queen Anne" to an eclectic, historically resonant style for modern houses. All the Galesburg houses, however, are excellent examples of the flourishing of the Queen Anne style in America.

Not open to the public, the private houses in the neighborhood form a unique collection of American architecture. Their setting, on spacious flat lots with gardens that seem to flow one into the other, is an archetype of the American small town, an image that conclusively formed in the popular imagination during this time, and remained firmly fixed for decades. ✺

Low-relief art tiles, featuring scenes from nature were particularly popular for decorating fireplaces.

OPPOSITE: *The Queen Anne house relied on rich color, both from its architectural elements like woodwork, and the favored decorations of the period.*

ELISA MICHAELS HOUSE, GALVESTON, TEXAS

AT THE TIME THE Queen Anne style emerged as a popular expression for American architecture, the "Queen City of the Gulf" was becoming one of the most affluent cities in America. This royal nickname was given to the city of Galveston on the Gulf Coast of Texas, a city that developed from a mere outpost on a strip of sand in the 1840s to a large and thriving shipping port by 1900.

Galveston was a natural business center for the region, with its confluence of seaport and railroads. It was also a major entry point for European immigrants coming to homestead in Texas and the Southwest. Serious fortunes were made in the busy port, particularly trans-shipping Texas cotton and grain; and in railroads and its attendant land development. During the 1870s to the 1890s, Galveston was at the height of its prominence and prosperity. The Strand, the oceanfront commercial area, became known as the "Wall Street of the Southwest" for its concentration of banking and insurance businesses.

The city's wealth was expressed in the construction of mansions up and down the island, a sort of Manhattan with better weather and beach views. Unlike the sober brick-and-brownstone row houses of northern banking centers, Galveston's architecture reflected the whimsy of a year-round beach community. Architecture was mainly wooden, and whatever decorative details that could be imagined were created and affixed to houses there. The biggest mansions and the smallest cottages appeared draped in lacy decoration, made of jig-sawn wood. Underneath the decoration, however, there were some practical considerations. The hot, sunny climate dictated a tropical approach—louvered shutters to keep the sun out but allow breezes through, and always, porches or verandas around the exterior to provide a sheltered place to enjoy the air and the view.

Galveston's residents embraced new technology, and boasted of the first telephone service (in 1878) and the first electric lights in Texas (in 1883). This progressive attitude toward domestic technology along with an embrace of historical styles as a source for design inspiration was typical of the period of ascendance of the Queen Anne style.

All of this turn-of-the-century joie-de-vivre was swept away when Galveston was devastated in a massive hurricane that swept ashore on September 8, 1900.

Thousands of people were killed; thousands more were left homeless; and the houses, stores, and port buildings were in ruins. Galveston vowed to rebuild, erecting a seawall to help protect the city, and embarking on a massive, eight-year project to raise the grade of the streets and properties throughout the city. All the surviving buildings were set on new foundations, and dredges poured four to six feet of sand beneath them. Many older houses were restored and saved from further storm damage, but the economy that had produced them in the first placed bypassed Galveston while it was rebuilding. The Houston Ship Channel was enlarged in 1914, taking Galveston's shipping industry to the growing city of Houston. Galveston became a quiet beach town, bypassed by the fierce urbanization that characterized prosperous twentieth century towns.

Today, many of the oldest surviving houses in Galveston are recognized as the East End Historic District, a residential area resplendent with the mansions, houses, and cottages of Galveston's boom time in the late nineteenth century. On Post Office Street, (named to commemorate the first post office in Texas, built in 1836), the Elisa Michaels House remains as a good example of the influence of the Queen

The main staircase is softly lighted from stained-glass windows.

Anne style on Gulf Coast architecture. Its original inhabitants were Sallie and Jacob Sonnentheil, their three children, and Sallie's mother, Elisa Michaels. Mrs. Michaels emigrated from Germany as a young woman; her first stop in the United States was Louisiana, where her daughter was born in 1856. They moved to Texas and joined the large German-born population that settled throughout the state in the latter nineteenth century. Her son-in-law, Jacob Sonnentheil, was himself a German immigrant. According to the Census of 1900, he was an insurance agent by trade. Firmly middle-class by standards both today and at the turn of the century, the family nevertheless had a live-in servant, an Irish woman named Bettie Brennan.[54]

Built in 1891, the house uses a traditional five-bay, center-hall plan, the simple box form used in American vernacular architecture since the eighteenth century. Sheathed in plain clapboard siding, the house lacks some of the textural richness usually associated with the style. In a nod to Galveston's climate, the projecting center gable shelters porches on both first and second floors, notable for the decorative wooden trim and complex railing pattern. A simple Georgian-classical dentil cornice encircles the house, but the applied decorative band above it on the gable ends, with a crossed pattern of miniature half-timbering and the incised quatrefoils in the porch trim offer medieval design references. The combination of these two stylistic vocabularies can only be indicative of the American Queen Anne style.

A well-preserved interior presents the layout, colors, and furnishing typical of the 1890s. Stained glass is present in several windows, some of it collected and installed in the house after the period of original construction. The center staircase is quite traditional and vernacular, like the plan of the house itself, and does not reflect the influence of the Queen Anne with its open plan and living-hall arrangements, but the turned balusters and the incised woodwork in a varnish finish in the stair hall reflect the prevailing taste of the time. The round-arched opening of the marbleized mantel is another decorative element of the house that was somewhat "old-fashioned" by 1891, but is brought up-to-date for the period when paired with the art-tile hearth. The extremely tall ceilings are a practical adaptation to the climate found in much vernacular architecture throughout the South. The present patterned wallpaper in the frieze and on the ceiling, while not original to the house, reflects the decorating trends most popular in the Queen Anne style.

The division of the wall into a main portion and upper frieze, wide openings between rooms,
and natural-toned woodwork with corner blocks marks this as a Queen Anne interior.

Stylized floral designs, or quatrefoils, punctuate the porch's cornice board.

Elisa Michaels' house represents the assimilation of the new Queen Anne style from an older building tradition. It is a somewhat modest, practical interpretation of the style, typical of the way people actually respond to new design ideas. The Sonnentheil's house survived the great hurricane of 1900, but the family did not, or at least not in Galveston. They drop from view from the public record after the Census of 1900, taken in the summer of that year before the hurricane struck. Their legacy is their house, one part of the larger historic district that shows the way a new American architectural style, the Queen Anne, came to be built across the country. ⁂

The small extension created by the bay window adds architectural interest to the parlor.

SHELTON–MCMURPHEY–JOHNSON HOUSE, EUGENE, OREGON

THE CITY OF EUGENE, Oregon, was founded in 1853 by Eugene Skinner, who also gave his name to the high hill rising up from the Willamette River, Skinner's Butte. Eugene Skinner's lumbering and trading center grew quickly, and within a generation, there was a commercial downtown at the base of the south side of the hill, and solid, fashionable houses began to rise above the downtown, replacing the earliest wooden cabins.

Through the last quarter of the nineteenth century, newcomers arrived in the new city every week, with hopes of making their fortune, of changing their luck, and of making a new life. Dr. Thomas Winthrop Shelton (1844–1893), a medical doctor, came to Eugene from the capital city, Salem, in 1884. Dr. Shelton had trained in San Francisco, so he had seen another, even bigger, city under development, and Shelton wanted to play his part in the development of Eugene. He established a medical practice, and also served as the local druggist. He became involved with local real estate, and understanding that development of any city was tied to the availability of a clean water supply, became an investor in Eugene's water utility. Success followed Dr. Shelton in all these ventures, and by 1886, he was ready to build the grandest house in Eugene, to secure the prominence of his family.

Dr. Shelton commissioned a young architect from Salem, Oregon, to design a house on property high on the hillside of Skinner's Butte, a commanding location from which all of downtown Eugene could be seen (and the doctor's house could be seen by the community). Walter D. Pugh, (1864–1935) had learned carpentry from his father, but by 1886 sought to distinguish himself from mere tradesmen, and boldly began to design buildings locally. Both Salem (population 3,300) and Eugene (population 1,200) were small towns in those days and it is likely that Shelton knew the Pugh family back in Salem, and was willing to give the son a chance at his chosen career of "architect."

The result is a rambling, Queen Anne–style house; as bold, as charming, and as unpolished as an ambitious young self-taught architect from Salem, Oregon. It combines pointed windows reminiscent of Gothic Revival–style architecture, a mansard roof from the Franco-Italianate style, and an extensive porch projecting the viewer over the valley below for dramatic views.

The entire structure was created in local woods, and it cost $7,000, a substantial investment in a house at a time when more-than-adequate suburban houses could be built for less than $3,000. Young Mr. Pugh relied on an experienced and well-regarded local builder, Nels Roney, to do the construction in 1887–1888. The partnership apparently worked, for Pugh and Roney, as architect and builder, collaborated later on Salem's City Hall and buildings on the University of Oregon campus in Eugene.

At the Shelton House, the date of completion is memorialized on the side of the house. The use of construction dates, applied decoratively to a house, appears in the Queen Anne style as part of the conscious historicizing idea of the building. Examples of "dated" contemporary buildings are found in the designs published in both pattern books and periodicals of the time. There is no evidence that Pugh received any formal training in architecture, or that he traveled abroad, so he must have relied on books and magazines from more cosmopolitan places for the ideas and images of currently fashionable domestic architecture that he incorporated into the Shelton House. The inclusion of the date on the side was but one clue that Pugh was looking carefully at published sources for his designs. The house did succeed in giving the Sheltons and Pugh a higher profile. The Shelton House remains the most elaborate example of the Queen Anne style in Eugene.

The house is painted green, with dark red trim, the original colors used in 1888. Wooden Queen Anne houses used a rich color palette for their exterior decoration, something again quite different from the English antecedents of the style. English Queen Anne architecture was generally red brick, with light-colored stone accents and white-painted trim. In America, wood was the most common building material, for structural members, trim, and decorative details, inside and out. Although brick color or "terra-cotta" was one popular paint color choice, the range of possibilities for exteriors ranged through browns, oranges, reds, golden-yellows, and greens. Only blue, which could still not be produced in a form stable to sunlight, would not have been used. At the Shelton House, the green color on the exterior also causes it to blend in with the evergreen forest that surrounds it, a visual nod to the aesthetic notions of the nineteenth century's most influential architectural tastemaker, A. J. Downing, who advised that houses should harmonize with their surroundings. The idea of blending house and landscape was further developed through the Victorian era, and so through the period, white was avoided, as it set the house off quite clearly from its landscape surroundings.

Although the Shelton House's irregular, asymmetrical profile lacks the precise balance achieved by the Watts Sherman House, or even the Roosevelt House, it is the fact that it incorporates so many visual elements of an emerging, contemporary style that makes it noteworthy. Here in little Eugene, Oregon, a decade after the first examples appeared in Newport and Philadelphia, more than 3,000 miles away, across a continent still contested by Indians in places, is a full-blown example of American Queen Anne architecture. It is a remarkable testament to the development, popularization, and widespread acceptance of a style of architecture that combined many disparate influences into a unique, national style.

Dr. Shelton did not live many years at his grand mansion—he died relatively young, at forty-nine, of leukemia. His only child, a daughter, Alberta, married at age twenty-one only a few months after her father's death. Her husband, Robert McMurphey, was an up-and-coming young man, who had already worked in the main offices of two railroads, and worked for an insurance company and real estate businesses. He was made superintendent of the Eugene water works, the utility Dr. Shelton had helped to found, and upon marrying Alberta, moved into the Shelton family house. Following their 1893 wedding, the McMurphey's regularly began to produce children, filling the Shelton–McMurphey house with six by 1904.

Louvered interior window shutters, pocket door, and the etched glass in the front transom are all typical of the Queen Anne style.

Built-in furnishings, particularly for dining rooms, first began to be developed during the Queen Anne style.

OPPOSITE: *The base of the front turret provides a cozy space for conversation and tea.*

Alberta Shelton–McMurphey loved music, and had studied at the local conservatory as a young woman. She worked, briefly, in a local photography studio prior to her marriage. Her interest in the arts extended throughout her life, and she contributed in her civic life to the improvement of education, the advancement of culture, and the promotion of beauty in Eugene. At her death in 1949, the grand dame of "The Castle on the Hill" was well known as one of the most influential women in the city.

After her death, the grand house she had grown up in and lived in throughout her adult life was sold, luckily to a couple who appreciated its history and architecture at a time when many Victorian-era houses were being destroyed as hopelessly old-fashioned. The Johnsons undertook a thorough restoration, and in 1986 the house passed to the City of Eugene. Now publicly owned and used as a museum and small meeting rooms, the house continues to overlook a city that evolved from a frontier town to a small city with a vital educational and commercial center. 🏵

The incised wooden columns frame the double doors and also the windows.

OPPOSITE: *Construction dates were occasionally incorporated into the design of a Queen Anne house.*

MILTON J. CARSON HOUSE, EUREKA, CALIFORNIA

THE CARSON HOUSE WAS commissioned about 1888 for William Carson, a pioneer to California who made a fortune in the lumber business. William gave the house to his son, Milton Carson, as a wedding present. The stylish Queen Anne house was occupied by Milton Carson and his wife, Minnie, and eventually their two daughters, Belle and Marion, for over thirty years.

Known today as "The Pink House" for its bright painted exterior—which is not its original color scheme—the Carson House represents the work of the Newsom Brothers, architect-builders whose work in the Queen Anne style brought it to the height of its West Coast development.

Samuel and Joseph Cather Newsom were born in Montreal, Canada, in the 1840s, but moved with their family, including ten siblings, to the outskirts of San Francisco in 1860. The 1870 Census records report that Samuel, at eighteen, the oldest still living at home, was working as an "appr[entice] to Architect."[55] He had joined his older brothers, John H. Newsom and Thomas D. Newsom, who were listed as "Architects and Superintendents of Building" in an 1873 San Francisco Directory.[56] The family architectural interest extended to at least one more, younger brother, Joseph Cather Newsom, who joined the practice in the mid-1870s. Age, experience, and perhaps temperament caused the firm to split—in 1878, the younger two, Samuel and Joseph, left to form their own architectural partnership, known as S & JC Newsom, which caused considerable confusion because the older brothers' firm, known as Newsom Brothers, Architects, remained in business as well.[57]

S & JC Newsom received a number of commissions and did quite well in San Francisco between the founding of their partnership in 1878 and 1885. At the conclusion of this period of their work, they brought out a pattern book, *Picturesque California Homes*, illustrating domestic designs, most of them in wood, that they had created. The book showed mostly Queen Anne–style houses, beginning with those with rather stiff, sticklike forms and gradually loosening into the turreted, gabled, and thoroughly decorated forms of mature American Queen Anne architecture. The book was astute public relations; a way to reach potential clients and the general public, making the Newsoms regionally well known as architects, and further popularizing their distinctive and exuberant rendition of the Queen Anne style.

In 1886, Joseph Cather Newsom, apparently the most ambitious of the brothers, left San Francisco to found an office in Los Angeles, where he was involved in several large-scale commercial projects. Although the brothers tried to collaborate long-distance, it was not surprising that the partnership broke up later that year. Samuel continued to work in San Francisco, and began to publish several pattern books, which included designs he and his brother had prepared prior to the firm's breakup, in addition to original work of his own. He developed the practice so that he produced designs for houses, then sold or published them, giving other architects and builders the opportunity to see the plans to completion. In this respect, Newsom was similar to his contemporaries George Barber in Tennessee, and the Palliser Brothers in Connecticut, who also offered Queen Anne designs by mail.

The long-standing attribution of the Carson House in Eureka to both Samuel and J. C. Newsom is therefore a bit difficult to prove. By the time the house was commissioned, the brothers were no longer in active partnership, but many designs they had worked on together were in circulation through pattern books. Elements of the Milton Carson House appear in other published work of the Newsoms, but the

Across the street from the Milton Carson House stands the house constructed by Samuel Newsom for Milton's father, William, in 1885.

entire house is an original composition, and one not presented to the public in the pattern books for copying. Was it an existing design from the brothers that was polished and finally built in 1888, or was it the creation of Samuel alone, but in the shadow of the reputation of the firm the brothers had created?

William Carson, who had this house built to give it to his son and daughter-in-law, had his own house constructed in 1885 to designs by Samuel Newsom alone. William Carson's house is one of the largest wooden mansions in America. It is a Stick–Style villa, a late example of a style that was a precursor to Queen Anne. The Newsoms were always boasting in their books and advertising materials that they were as up-to-date as possible. Both brothers have attributed work in the Stick Style, Queen Anne style, Colonial Revival, and later, Beaux-Arts style, following the progression of architectural styles that rolled across America in rapid succession from the 1870s to the early 1900s. However, they remained historicists in the way they understood style, clothing basic forms in various decorative coverings. A twentieth-century historian notes that architects were described as being "so caught up in the flurry of various fashion changes in ornament and materials that they were incapable of joining the great mainstream of local carpentry and anonymous design which eventually led to a form of modern architecture in the 1890's."[58] The Bay Area modernism that began in the early 1900s with the work of Greene & Greene (another architecture firm of brothers) and Bernard Maybeck, work that relied on pure form and no ornament, was never to be explored by the Newsoms.

In any event, the Milton Carson House shows an assured designer at work, one who knew the Queen Anne style and who was familiar with working in northern California's native material, redwood. The Milton Carson House is a modest-sized house compared to that of his father, but it has all the elements of a grand mansion packed into its compact footprint. The asymmetrical façade is divided in the gable front, incorporating a two-story bay window, and the rounded, corner tower, topped with a curving, onion-dome roof. The lacy-looking wooden trim extends from the projecting portico of the front porch to the arcaded screen supporting a second-floor balcony. The columns on the porch are deeply turned and incised, and the same turned wood detail enriches pendant drops from the top of the bargeboard. The neoclassical architectural language is introduced into the house through a wide frieze circling the tower, and the graceful applied pediment over the gable window.

Entirely wooden, the house's siding is varied from location to location, covering the exterior entirely with different textures. From the relatively simple beaded, horizontally laid boards, which suggest a

The main staircase and front hall have uniquely profiled balusters and newel post.

Intricately layered and detailed geometric designs create a richness of texture and design from the peak of the house down to the siding at the lowest level.

masonry course at the basement level, the wall surfaces change to a grooved clapboard on the first floor, and diamond-pattern shingles, both square-cut and hexagonally cut shingles, laid in staggered patterns on the second floor. In the gables, the wooden shingles form wavy patterns or rows of fish-scale shingles. Similarly, all the trim work is ornamented with "buttons," or incising, or other ornamentation. Taken together this wooden relief gives richness to the exterior that is really extraordinary, well above and beyond most American Queen Anne constructions.

It could be the Carson House that Gilette Burgess, a Boston-bred editor of the San Francisco weekly, *The Wave*, was writing about when he penned:

> [The ideal Queen Anne house] "…should have a conical corner-tower, it should be built of at least three incongruous materials, or better, imitations thereof; it should have its window openings absolutely haphazard; it should represent parts of every known and unknown order of architecture; it should be so plastered with ornament as to conceal the theory of its construction; it should be a restless, uncertain, frightful collection of details, giving the effect of a nightmare about to explode.[59]

Burgess was a humorist—he is most famous as the author of the little poem that begins, "I never saw a purple cow…" He was also an illustrator by training, and this comic lambasting of popular architecture was done by someone who had really looked at the new buildings in the Queen Anne style springing up around town. The Newsoms' buildings were enriched with so much detail that the parts do tend to overtake an appreciation of the whole. Truthfulness of construction was the least important architectural objective to the Newsoms, although the notion was gaining currency at the end of the nineteenth century with the emerging modernists. The criticism leveled by Burgess and others of the decorative excesses of the Queen Anne style were not without merit, but the accomplished Baroque interpretation of the style that appears in the Carson House and other works of the Newsom Brothers is true to itself. The Newsoms' houses were created by and for an American public fascinated with technology, and the overwhelming presence of machine-made detail supports that. It may also be that the public's determination to create a native architecture that reflected the many diverse cultures and peoples who came together to form America also has an expression in this architecture of inclusion, where every element from past times and locations has a place.

Inside, the house is richly detailed with a grand staircase, lined by a paneled wainscot. The hall includes stained-glass windows in bright colors, which bring warmth to the interior yet provide privacy in this densely-developed neighborhood. As prescribed by the decorators of the period, even the ceiling is enriched with ornament, and like the exterior, it is the three-dimensional aspects of design that provide the most interest.

The house was restored in the late 1960s for office use, and it remains in private ownership today. 🐚

TOP: *Ceiling moldings and center medallion show all surfaces were designed and decorated for maximum impact.*

BOTTOM: *Staircase detail inside the Milton Carson House.*

OPPOSITE: *The period-appropriate hall piece is scaled for the baronial living halls and entries of the Queen Anne–style house.*

PIATT HOUSE, TUNKHANNOCK, PENNSYLVANIA

ONE OF THE MOST POPULAR and successful of late nineteenth-century America's architect-builders was George Franklin Barber. Barber was a self-taught Midwesterner, born in Illinois in 1854. He moved to Kansas as a boy, returned to Illinois as a young man and then settled in the mountains of East Tennessee in 1888. In that time he learned farming, specialized in raising "ornamental nursery stock," pursued rock collecting with a passion, and apprenticed to his older brother as a carpenter. And apparently he also devoured whatever books and magazines about building, architecture, and design came into his hands.

From their popular introduction in the 1840s in America, pattern books, or books of architectural designs (chiefly domestic and suburban in tone), increased in number through the nineteenth century. Produced by architects, or architect-builders, they promoted the talent of the authors, and the current architectural fashions to an American middle-class audience. It was undoubtedly through pattern books that young George Barber learned about popular architecture in the 1870s and 80s as he pursued his carpentry work. But he aspired not just to build, but to design, and so to advertise his talents in this area, he created a small publication he titled *The Cottage Souvenir, Eighteen Engravings of Houses Ranging in Price from $900.00 to $8000.00 in Wood, Brick and Stone, Artistically Combined* (1887). Published in DeKalb, Illinois, where he was working at the time, the small paperback showed houses utterly typical for their time and place—simplified versions of Gothic Revival and Stick Style designs, trying to express themselves as the Queen Anne style, but still too vertical, too tightly planned, and too plain to really achieve characterization in that style.

By 1891, he published a much more substantial book, *The Cottage Souvenir No. 2, A Repository of Artistic Cottage Architecture and Miscellaneous Designs*, which was available hardbound or in paperback. It circulated to a national audience, and was calculated to promote Barber as much as his designs. In the introductory text he wrote:

> Before you begin to build, be sure you have secured the very best plans and design that you can obtain for the price. Correspond with architects and designers until you have found just what you want. Do not be afraid of offending some one. When you have secured your plans and perfected your details, get the best mechanic you can find to do the work.[60]

Thus from Knoxville, Tennessee, George Barber became a national architect, not because he traveled, but because his plans did. People looked at his pattern books, decided on a design that suited them, wrote to Barber for the full plans, perhaps with changes to accommodate a particular family or an oddly-laid out lot. Barber (and his growing staff) created a set of working plans, which were mailed off to be executed by a local builder. As a former carpenter, Barber was sensitive to their needs and noted in his text for *Cottage Souvenir No. 2*, "Knowing, as I do, that my working drawings, when they leave the office, go out of reach of my personal supervision, I have taken especially pains to make everything plain and easily understood by mechanics generally. Every detail that goes from the office is full size and drawn by hand (not printed)."[61]

The mail-order plan from a catalog was not an innovation of Barber's—George Palliser of Bridgeport, Connecticut, takes credit for the concept as early as 1876. R. W. Shoppell in New York produced monthly magazines under the name the Co-operative Building Plan Association in the 1880s, which also sold building plans through correspondence between far-off clients and a pool of architects.

George Barber, a builder and self-taught architect, promoted his design business nationally.

George Barber's books circulated among a wide audience, and an audience that was willing not only to purchase the book, but also to buy the plans, and eventually build from them.

A magazine for the craftsman and contractor, *The Builder and Woodworker*, noted the need for ready-made plans: "Every village builder should always have a large number of elevations and plans of cottages, barns, and stables on hand, he should be able to tell the cost of any one of these cottages, etc, etc, when finished at once. This would assist him to get many contracts he might otherwise lose if he was not provided with plans and information when wanted."[62] In the case of the Piatt House in Pennsylvania, we know it was the family who purchased the plans and then selected a contractor; in other instances it was an enterprising builder who purchased plans, erected a house, and enticed a buyer with a design of the most up-to-date fashion.

Barber's designs enjoyed some popularity because they were typical of the emerging Queen Anne–domestic architectural style of the late nineteenth century, and because he added unique and exuberant touches to his houses. The larger the house, of course, the more complicated in form and plan, but even modest houses by Barber incorporated whimsical details such as elaborate bargeboard trim around gables and turrets, a second floor porch or balcony, perhaps a small round window over the stairs, or a horse-shoe arch. Utterly free of experience with genuine English Queen Anne–style buildings or the academic teachings of formal American architectural education, Barber's designs are the exuberant fantasy of millwork, turrets and porches that form the pinnacle of the American style.

Barber's directions for constructing a house were thorough, and covered practical as well as aesthetic concerns. As he notes in his introduction to *New Model Dwellings*, "All plans (unless otherwise noted) are prepared for stone foundation; good frost-proof cellar, 7 feet deep; sheathing and paper for all outside walls, when house is frame; shingled roof; three coats of paint and plaster; a good quality of glass and hardware; two rooms and hall in hardwood, except for houses of low cost. In fact, everything is figured for a complete job well finished."[63]

The Piatt House, built in 1896, shows the full extent of Barber's talent as designer and builder, and the audience who responded to him. The house is exceptionally well preserved in private hands, and its construction is well-documented. The design for the house was published in Barber's update of *The Cottage Souvenir*, published as *New Model Dwellings and How Best to Build Them*, in 1895–1895. Design 56B in that edition showed a massive house on a corner lot, the street corner enlivened by a second-floor tower with a distinct conical roof. Deep porches wrapped the first floor, and a small porch also projected from the second floor at the side of the house. Cresting and pinnacles gave the roofline a most irregular line; indeed the Barber catalog titled the design "A Picturesque Home."

Stairs cascade past the decorative newel post on the main staircase.

Barber in fact never uses the term "Queen Anne" in any descriptive material in all of *New Model Dwellings*. Rather, he called his house designs "picturesque" or "artistic" or "modern." The text accompanying the description of Design 56B calls the house "Romanesque":

> **A Picturesque House:** On page 73, we show a design for a ten-room residence in the Romanesque style. It has five rooms on the first floor, with a convenient reception hall and a front veranda, both artistic in appearance and varied in plan, which will be found a very delightful feature. Glass, hardware, and plumbing are all good. This house, when properly built and painted in appropriate tints, will present a beautiful appearance. The design and general proportions are in good keeping. Estimated cost to build $6000 to $6400. Price of complete plans and specifications, $80.00. Size 47 x 71 feet.[64]

James W. Piatt (1850–1914) owned a brick house on a level corner lot in the small town of Tunkhannock, Pennsylvania. From there he could easily walk to the Wyoming County Courthouse and to the small downtown, where he was active in legal matters for his entire career. He and his wife, Frances, had one daughter, Eulalie Mae (1878–1980). When Eulalie was eighteen, the family moved to their summer house, on Lake Carey just outside of town, while the brick house was demolished, and construction began on the new one, Design 56B in *New Model Dwellings* by George Barber.

The pattern book estimate for the price of the house is given at $6,500, putting it at the high end of Barber's published designs. It is unknown how much the house finally cost, but Piatt did pay additional costs for upgrades to the specified woodwork and windows. Estimates for these items were prepared on April 22, 1896, and included a notation for a front door of quarter-sawn oak with plate glass in the top and beveled panels at the base. The interior sliding doors for first-floor rooms were of ash, while the majority of the doors were to be western pine. Doors $225.00; the fifty-eight windows in the house, including several of "art glass" would cost an additional $383.00. It appears from inspection of the house today that the estimate for doors was accepted, but the windows were rethought, reducing the number in "art glass."

The contractors and the millwork for the Piatt House were from Wilkes-Barre, a much larger town south of Tunkhannock. Eleven workmen arrived in July 1896; the work was completed three months later and the family moved in November 20, 1896. Such speed of construction reflects both a well-designed and carefully planned project, and the clear experience of the firm of W. H. Shepherd & Son, who were well-known contractors and lumber dealers in the Wilkes-Barre and Scranton, Pennsylvania area in the late nineteenth and early twentieth century.

Soon after the Piatt family moved in, Eulalie went off to Wellesley College, graduating in 1901. She followed her father, and her grandfather, into law, and was one of the first women attorneys in Pennsylvania. She practiced in Tunkhannock and lived in the big house with her parents, and remained there even after her marriage at age thirty-two to Joseph F. Ogden, also an attorney, a veteran of the Spanish American War, and a director of the local bank. They had just one child, a son, James P. Ogden, born in 1919.

The house remained in the hands of the original family until 1971, a family who did not do much to change anything inside or out. After it was sold out of the family, it embarked on a perilous time, its size and location making it a target for commercial reuse and much harder wear and tear than it had known previously. But in 1995, new owners, appreciating the house's Queen Anne style, restored it to its original splendor and today it is once again the grandest house in town.

Stained and leaded glass decorate the front entry.

Extraordinary tile work featuring lilies highlights this double-tiered fireplace mantel.

A local millwork company created woodwork for the house, and each fireplace within the house has a different design.

The front bedroom of the Piatt House.

OPPOSITE: *The butler's pantry provided efficient workspace.*

From the front, the house projects toward the street, each gable and porch and turret reaching out to the passersby on the old slate sidewalk. The deep semicircular porch is expressed as a distinct exterior room, as indeed it was, furnished with carpets, chairs, and potted plants in a photo of Eulalie Mae Piatt. The main entrance to the house is marked by the low pediment over a broad flight of stairs, clearly articulating the entry, but sheltering the door itself in deep shadow, so that visitors were well protected from the elements as they made their way to the front door, and nosy neighbors could not clearly see who, in fact, was visiting.

The triple windows across the second floor façade have a nearly circular transom of art glass above them, giving the appearance from the exterior of a series of exotic, Arabic or Syrian arches. The delight in the exotic is also seen around the side of the house, where the porch off the master bedroom uses a curving arch form reminiscent of the Middle East. Of course all this is set under half-timbered gables and accented with cornice appliqués in a neo-classical swag motif. These unique, cross-cultural details are particularly associated with George Barber, but were of course also the hallmark of the American Queen Anne style.

Mr. Piatt was a well-to-do, well-educated man from a prominent local family. He might have hired a trained architect from the nearby cities of Scranton or Wilkes-Barre to design his new house, but one suspects that he and his family liked the exuberance of design that Barber's book presented. Perhaps money came into the equation, but the amount spent on the house as built by the Piatts would have accommodated architects' fees, had they been desired. The Piatts were aspiring to the most ostentatious house in town, a clear embodiment of their own success, and Barber's design represented that for them, as for many of their countrymen, in the 1890s.

The interior of the house is an essay in American wood and woodworking skills of the late nineteenth century—appropriate enough for a town in the wooded hills of Pennsylvania where lumbering was a dominant industry. The front entry leads to an asymmetrical hall, dominated by the chestnut-paneled staircase lighted by an arched window of stained glass. Unlike many Queen Anne–style houses, the entry itself does not have a fireplace, but the stair window, windows in the front door, and a projecting bay window fitted with a cozy window seat flood the entry with light.

A long parlor laid out crosswise through the center of the house offered entertaining space for the family, a place to showcase fine furnishings, play music, and carry on all the parlor games and conversation the Victorian era was famous for. Sliding double doors of oak separated the parlor from the wood-paneled study. The dining room to the rear of the parlor is the only room whose fireplace has been replaced since original construction, but it is perfectly in keeping with the style that might have been used.

A pantry, with low wooden counter and copper sink between walls lined with shelves, gave the staff of the house extra capacity to serve meals to the family and their guests, and prevented direct connection between the dining room and the kitchen, to spare diners the heat and odors of the kitchen. Queen Anne houses, including the best ones by pattern-book authors, acknowledged the interest in sanitation and hygiene by separating functions within a house to the fullest extent possible. As Barber wrote in *New Model Dwellings*, "Building a house is no trifle; the health and life of your family depend upon the care and good judgement [sic] you use in the matter . . . you can here either sacrifice or increase the comfort and happiness of all concerned."[65]

The happiness of the Piatt family was, no doubt, increased by the spacious bedrooms on the second floor, with a bathroom including tub, water closet, and sink located at the end of a long hall. A narrow, twisting back stair connects the kitchen on the first floor with servants' rooms on the third floor. The main staircase also ascends to the third floor, where in the front of the house is a billiard room. The high ceiling reflects the complicated roofline that rises above, and gives the room a feeling of spaciousness far beyond its square footage.

The Piatt House is a wonderful expression of the American Queen Anne style, and a vivid illustration of the influence of books in the transmission of architectural ideas to the home-building public in the late nineteenth century. 🌸

BIBLIOGRAPHY OF THE STYLE

ON THE ENGLISH ORIGINS OF THE QUEEN ANNE STYLE

Girouard, Mark. *Sweetness and Light: The Queen Anne Movement, 1860–1900*. New Haven, Connecticut: Yale University Press, 1984.

ON THE AMERICAN ORIGINS OF THE QUEEN ANNE STYLE

Scully, Jr., Vincent J. *The Shingle Style and The Stick Style*. New Haven, Connecticut: Yale University Press, Revised Edition 1971.

Scully, Vincent. Introduction, *The Architecture of the American Summer: The Flowering of the Shingle Style*. The Temple Hoyne Buell Center for the Study of American Architecture, Columbia University, The City of New York: Documents of American Architecture Series, General Editor Robert A. M. Stern. New York: Rizzoli International Publications, Inc., 1989.

ON INTERIORS:

Cook, Clarence. *The House Beautiful: Essays on Beds and Tables, Stools and Candlesticks. 2nd Edition*, New York: Charles Scribners and Sons, 1881. Reprinted by Dover Publications, New York, 1995.

Eastlake, Charles. *Hints on Household Taste in Furniture, Upholstery and Other Details*. 4th Edition, London: Longmans, Green & Co., 1878. Reprinted by Dover Publications, New York, 1969.

PATTERN BOOKS WITH ELEVATIONS, PLANS AND DETAILS

Barber, George. *The Cottage Souvenir No. 2: A Repository of Artistic Cottage Architecture*. Knoxville, Tennessee: S. B. Newman & Co., 1891. Reprinted by Dover Publications, New York, 2004. The introduction by Michael A. Tomlan entitled "Toward the Growth of an Artistic Taste" is included in this reprint edition; it is from an earlier reprinting of *The Cottage Souvenir No. 2* by the American Life Foundation and Study Institute, Watkins Glen, New York, 1982.

Cirker, Blanche, ed., *Victorian House Designs in Authentic Full Color: 75 Plates* from the "Scientific American—Architects and Builders Edition" 1885–1894. New York: Dover Publications, 1986.

Comstock, William T. Modern *Architectural Designs and Details*. William T. Comstock, Pulisher, New York, 1881. Reprinted by Dover Publications as *Victorian Domestic Architectural Plans and Details*, 1987.

Palliser, Palliser & Co., Architects, *American Architecture, or Every Man a Complete Builder*. J. S. Ogilve, Publisher, New York, 1888. Reprinted by American Life Foundation with a new Introduction by Michael Tomlan, 1978.

Reed, S. B. *Dwellings for Village and Country*. New York: Orange Judd Company, 1885. Reprinted by Dover Publications as *Victorian Dwellings for Village and Country*, 1999.

Shoppell, Robert W. et. al. *Building Designs*, R. W. Shoppell, Publisher, New York, ca. 1890. Reprinted by *Dover Publications as Turn-of-the Century Houses, Cottage and Villas*, 1983.

FOR MORE INFORMATION ON ARCHITECTS MENTIONED IN SPECIFIC CHAPTERS

Blomfield, Sir Reginald. *Richard Norman Shaw, RA. Architect*, 1831–1912, London: B. T. Batsford, Ltd, 1940.

Thomas, George E., Michael S. Lewis, and Jeffrey Cohen, *Frank Furness: The Complete Works*. New York: Princeton Architectural Press, NY, 1991.

Storrer, William Allin. *The Architecture of Frank Lloyd Wright: A Complete Catalog, 3rd Edition*. Chicago: University of Chicago Press, 2002.

VENTILATING REGISTERS.
SCALE ¼ FULL SIZE.

CUT BRASS VENTILATING REGISTER IN SPANDRIL.

SCALE ⅓ FULL SIZE

VENTILATING REGISTERS IN SPANDRILS

SCALE ⅓ FULL SIZE.

J. P. Putnam, Architect. Boston.

NOTES

INTRODUCTION

1 *The Brooklyn Daily Eagle*, Brooklyn, New York, September 21, 1884, page 3.

2 *The Brooklyn Daily Eagle*, Brooklyn, New York, April 16, 1899, page 31.

3 *The American Builder*, June 1876, page 302.

4 *The American Architect and Building News*, December 16, 1876, page 405.

5 *The Builder and Woodworker*, September 1880, page 178.

6 *Palliser's New Cottage Homes and Details*. New York: Palliser, Palliser & Co., 1887, Preface.

7 *The American Architect and Building News*, June 28, 1879, page 207.

8 *Palliser's New Cottage Homes and Details*, Palliser, Palliser & Co., New York, 1887, text to plate 39.

9 John D. Crane, "The Decorative Use of Color." *Building: An Architectural Weekly*, Vol. 8, June 23, 1888, page 202.

10 Charles Thomas Davis. *Manufacture of Bricks, Tiles and Terra-Cotta*. London: Sampson Low, Marston, Searle and Rivington, 1886, pages 425–426.

11 Hans Van Lemmen. *Tiles: 1,000 Years of Architectural Decoration*. New York: Harry N. Abrams, 1993, pages 168–172.

12 George Palliser, *New Cottage Homes and Details*, New York, 1887, introductory page, not numbered.

13 S. B. Reed. *Dwellings for Village and Country*. New York: Orange Judd & Company, 1885, page 101.

14 "On Health and Comfort in House Building," *The Builder*, London, Vol. 31, August 23, 1873, page 669.

15 Kenneth M. Wilson. "Window Glass in America," Building Early America, The Carpenters' Company of the city and county of Philadelphia, 1976, pages 157–158, 161.

16 *The American Architect and Building News*, February 17, 1877, pages 54–55.

17 "Chambers in Leadenhall Street, London," *The Builder*, London, Volume 31, August 2, 1873.

18 George F. Barber. *The Cottage Souvenir No. 2*. Knoxville, Tenn.: S. B. Newman & Co., 1891, page 8.

19 Lonard D. Hosford. "How to Plumb a Suburban House" in *Suburban and Country Houses*. New York: William Comstock, 1893, pages 15–22.

20 George F. Barber. *New Model Dwellings and How Best to Build Them*. Knoxville, Tenn.: George Barber & Co., Architects, 1895–1896, from the Introduction.

21 Ernest Peixotto. Quoted by David Gebhard in "Samuel and Joseph Cather Newsome-Architects," *Victorian Architectural Imagery in California 1878–1908*. Exhibition catalog, University of California at Santa Barbara Arts Museum, 1979, page 13.

22 *The Brooklyn Daily Eagle*, April 16, 1899, page 31.

23 *The American Architect and Building News*, June 10, 1876, page 187.

24 *The American Architect and Building News*, March 24, 1877, page 93.

25 Robert Swain Peabody. "A Talk About Queen Anne," *The American Architect and Building News*, Vol. II, No. 70, April 28, 1877, page 134.

26 Robert Shoppell, *How to Build, Furnish and Decorate*, The Co-operative Building Plan Association, New York, 1883.

William B. Tuthill, *Interiors and Interior Details: fifty-two large quarto plates, comprising a large number of original designs of halls, staircases, parlors, libraries, dining rooms, &c.* New York: William T. Comstock, 1882.

27 Clarence Cook. *The House Beautiful*. New York: Charles Scribner and Sons, 1881, page 22.

28 Ibid, page 190.

29 John D. Crane, "The Decorative Use of Color," *Building: An Architectural Weekly*. Vol. 8, June 23, 1888, pages 201–202.

30 Clarence Cook. *The House Beautiful*, New York: Charles Scribner and Sons, 1881,

31 Ibid, page 334.

32 Charles Eastlake. *Hints on Household Taste*, London: Longmans, Green and Company, 1878, reprinted Dover Publications 1969, page 123.

ROOSEVELT HOUSE, SAGAMORE HILL

33 Montgomery Schuyler. "Recent Buildings in New York." *Harper's New Monthly Magazine* 67, no. 300, September, 1883, pages 557–78.

34 Theodore Roosevelt, 1883, quoted in the Sagamore Hill Website, www.theodore-roosevelt.com/trsahi.html, accessed November 7, 2004.

EDWARD BROOKE HOUSE

35 From "Self-Reliance," an essay written by Ralph Waldo Emerson in 1839–1840.

CASTLE HILL

36 *New York Times*, September 15, 1898, page 7.

37 Vincent J. Scully, Jr. *The Shingle Style and The Stick Style*. Revised edition. New Haven, Connecticut: Yale University Press, 1971.

38 *The Washington Post*, April 7, 1910, page 15.

CHARLES BALDWIN HOUSE

39 Charles Handy Russell (1796–1884), Scrapbook, Volume III, page 139, Newport Historical Society, Vault A. "Newport—Extensive Improvements Going on in the fashionable Seaside Resort," March 26, 1878. This article is fully quoted in the Historic American Buildings Survey documentation for the Charles H. Baldwin House, HABS no. RI-334, prepared under the direction of James C. Massey, Chief of HABS, 1970. Available through http://memory.loc.gov/pnp/habshaer/ri/rio300/rio323/data/007.gif.

HARTFORD STREET

40 Cook, Clarence. *The House Beautiful*. New York: Charles Scribner and Sons, 1881, page 113.

CENTRE STREET

41 Frampton, Kenneth. *Modern Architecture: A Critical History*, revised edition. London: Thames & Hudson Publishers, 1985, page 46.

PROSPECT STREET

42 R. W. Shoppell. *Turn-of-the-Century Houses, Cottages and Villas: Floor Plans and Line Illustrations of 118 Homes from Shoppell's Catalogs*. New York: Dover Publications, 1983, page 119.

43 Charles L. Eastlake. *Hints on Household Taste*. London: Longmans, Green and Company, 1878, reprinted Dover Publications 1969, page 136.

44 Clarence Cook, *The House Beautiful*: Essays on Beds and Tables Stools and Candlesticks. New York: Charles Scribner and Sons, 1881, reprinted Dover Publications, 1995, pages 277–278.

WILLIAM E. CONOVER HOUSE

45 *Scientific American Architects and Builders Edition*, May 1890, page 79.

HAAS–LILIENTHAL HOUSE

46 In the mid-nineteenth century San Francisco was acknowledged as one of the least anti-Semitic cities in the United States, perhaps because of its relatively recent founding, its inclusive boomtown origins, and the fact that almost half of its population was in fact Jewish. The Gold Rush and the booming development of San Francisco coincided exactly with the failed revolutions in Germany of 1848, which led to the emigration of large numbers of German Jews.

47 From the *San Francisco Newsletter*, June 25, 1888; reprinted in *Victorian Classics of San Francisco*, a reprinting of the 1888 edition of Artistic Homes of California, with an introduction by Alex Brammer; published by Windgate Press, Sausalito, California, 1987.

48 *Artistic Homes of California*, description of the "Residence of Mr. William Haas," opposite plate 30.

49 Ibid.

50 Ibid.

JOHN LINDALE HOUSE

51 Twelfth United States Census, East—South Murderkill Hundred, Village of Magnolia, Kent County, Delaware, 1900, page 51 of 55.

KRABBENHOFT FARMHOUSE

52 *Moorhead Independent*, Moorhead North Dakota, July 19, 1901 and August 2, 1901. From a private collection.

OVIDE BROUSSARD HOUSE

53 Twelfth United States Census, Abbeville, Vermillion Parish, Louisiana, page 9A.

ELISA MICHAELS HOUSE

54 Twelfth United States Census, Galveston, Texas.

CARSON HOUSE

55 Ninth Census of the United States, 1870, for the town of Brooklyn, Alameda County, California.

56 David Gebhard, *Samuel and Joseph Cather Newsom—Architect: Victorian Architectural Imagery in California, 1878–1908.* Exhibition catalog, University of California at Santa Barbara Arts Museum, 1979. Local History collection of San Francisco Public Library.

57 Ibid, pages 15–17.

58 Joseph A. Baird. *Historic American Buildings Survey Documentation for the Carson House* (HABS – CAL 12-EUR 6), Library of Congress, 1964 and available through http://hdl.loc.gov/loc.pnp/hhh.ca0174.

59 From the collection of the San Francisco Architectural Heritage Foundation. Used with permission.

PIATT HOUSE

60 George Barber. *The Cottage Souvenir No. 2.* Knoxville, Tennessee: S. B. Newman & Co., Steam Book and Job Printer, 1891, page 4.

61 Ibid, pages 10–11.

62 *The Builder and Woodworker*, Charles Lakey, New York, Vol. I, No. 4, April 1880, page 67.

63 George Barber. *New Model Dwellings and How Best to Build Them.* Knoxville, Tenn.: George Barber & Co., Architects, 1895–1896, page 5.

House of Uriah Coffin, Boston, Massachusetts, 1879. From The American Architect and Building News, *October 18, 1879. Reproduced with permission from Avery Architectural and Fine Arts Library.*

ACKNOWLEDGMENTS

The on-line listing of places recorded since the 1930s for the Historic American Buildings Survey available through the Library of Congress affords the architectural researcher an opportunity to look around the country for examples of the Queen Anne style, and see plans and photographs of many great houses in the style.

Listings of properties on the National Register of Historic Places, which in some states are now available on the internet through the good work of State Historic Preservation Offices, also brings information on far-off places into the study of the researcher.

With sincerest thanks to all who opened their homes for inspection, shared history and tea with the author and the photographer, and who work daily to maintain and preserve Queen Anne architecture in America. A special "thank you" to the extreme generosity of Chuck & Ellen McWithy and to Bob and Barb Arnoldini for sharing particular family photographs, histories, and mementoes.

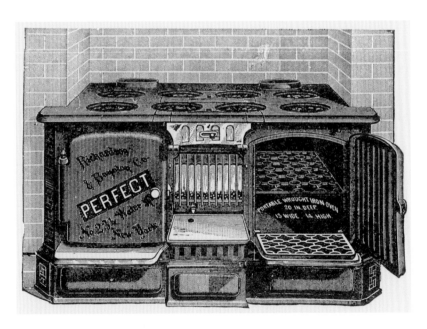

Advertisement for the "Perfect" stove, from advertising placed in the back of New Cottage Homes and Details *by Palliser, Palliser, & Co., Architects, New York, 1887. Reprinted by the American Life Foundation, 1978.*

PHOTOGRAPH CREDITS

All photos by Radek Kurzaj unless otherwise noted.

INTRODUCTION

PAGE 10
Residence of C. W. Van Slyke, published in *The American Architect and Building News*, November 13, 1880. Reproduced with permission from Avery Architectural and Fine Arts Library.

PAGE 12
"Grim's Dyke," published in *Richard Norman Shaw, Architect*, by Reginald Blomfield. Reproduced with permission from Avery Architectural and Fine Arts Library.

PAGE 14
Frontispiece of *The American Architect and Building News*, Vol. VII, 1880. Reproduced with permission from Avery Architectural and Fine Arts Library.

PAGE 15
The British Building at the 1876 Centennial Exposition, Philadelphia. Photo ca. 1876; photographer unknown. Reproduced with permission from the Free Library of Philadelphia.

PAGE 16
"Leyswood," published in *Richard Norman Shaw, Architect*, by Reginald Blomfield. Reproduced with permission from Avery Architectural and Fine Arts Library.

PAGE 17
"Cottage at Newport for W. Watts Sherman, Esq.," from *The New-York Sketch-Book of Architecture*, Vol. II, No. V, February 1875, Plate XVIII. Reproduced with permission from Avery Architectural and Fine Arts Library.

PAGE 19
From William T. Comstock, *Modern Architectural Designs and Details*, 1881. Reprinted by Dover Publications as *Victorian Domestic Architectural Plans and Details*, 1987.

PAGE 20
From *Scientific American—Architect's and Builders Edition*, April 1890. Reproduced with permission from Avery Architectural and Fine Arts Library.

PAGE 21
From *Scientific American—Architect's and Builders Edition*, June 1886. Reprinted by Dover Publications as *Victorian Designs in Authentic Full Color*, 1996.

PAGE 22
From advertising placed in the back of *New Cottage Homes and Details*, by Palliser, Palliser & Co., Architects, New York, 1887. Reprinted by The American Life Foundation, 1978.

PAGE 25
From William T. Comstock, *Modern Architectural Designs and Details*, 1881. Reprinted by Dover Publications as *Victorian Domestic Architectural Plans and Details*, 1987.

PAGE 26
From Architecture and Building Magazine, December 5, 1891. Reproduced with permission from Avery Architectural and Fine Arts Library.

PAGE 29
From advertising placed in the back of *New Cottage Homes and Details*, by Palliser, Palliser & Co., Architects, New York, 1887. Reprinted by The American Life Foundation, 1978.

PAGE 31
From William B. Tuthill's *Interiors and Interior Details*, 1882

PAGE 32
Courtesy Chuck and Ellen McWethy, Sabin, Minnesota.

PAGE 33
Frontispiece from Clarence Cook's *The House Beautiful*, 1881, reprinted by Dover Publications, 1995.

PAGE 34
From Clarence Cook's *The House Beautiful*, 1881, reprinted by Dover Publications, 1995.

PAGE 35
LEFT: From *The American Architect and Building News*, December 4, 1880.
RIGHT: Reproduced with permission from Avery Architectural and Fine Arts Library.

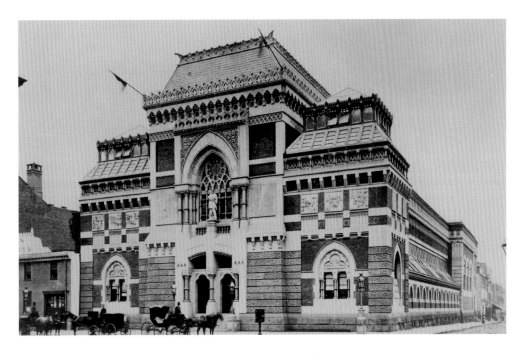

Pennsylvania Academy of the Fine Arts, designed by Frank Furness, 1876–1877.

WATTS SHERMAN

PAGE 44

"Interior Perspective of Hall" in the Watts Sherman House, *New-York Sketch-Book of Architecture*, Vo. II, No. V, May 1875, Plate XIX. Reproduced with permission from Avery Architectural and Fine Arts Library.

PAGE 57

Frederick Gutekunst, photographer. Pennsylvania Academic of the Fine Arts, 1876-77. Albumen print. Courtesy of the Pennsylvania Academy of the Fine Arts, Philadelphia, Archives.

BALDWIN HOUSE

PAGE 78

C. H. Baldwin House illustration from *The American Architect and Building News*, March 23, 1878. Reproduced with permission from Avery Architectural and Fine Arts Library.

SUBURBAN HOUSES

PAGE 84

Bedford Park from a hand-tinted illustration, ca. 1882, published as a series showing the R. N. Shaw development. Classics collection, Avery Architectural and Fine Arts Library. Reprinted with permission from Avery Architectural and Fine Arts Library.

PROSPECT STREET

PAGE 110

From Shoppell's *Modern Houses*, 1890, reprinted as *Turn-of-the-Century-Houses, Cottages and Villas* by Dover Publications, 1984.

WILLIAM E. CONOVER HOUSE

PAGE 135

Scientific American Architects and Builder's Edition, May 1890. Reprinted with permission from Avery Architectural and Fine Arts Library.

KRABBENHOFT FARMHOUSE

PAGE 173

Images courtesy Chuck and Ellen McWethy, Sabin, Minnesota.

PAGE 175

"Overseer's House" at Magnolia Plantation, Natchitoches Parish, Louisiana. Library of Congress, Prints and Photographs Division, Historic American Buildings Survey, HABS, LA, 35-NATCH, v-2.

PIATT HOUSE

PAGE 216

Historic photos of the Piatt House used with permission by Mr. and Mrs. Robert Arnoldini.

PAGE 233

Frederick Gutekunst, photographer. Pennsylvania Academic of the Fine Arts, 1876–1877. Albumen print. Courtesy of the Pennsylvania Academy of the Fine Arts, Philadelphia Archives.

FEATURES ON AN AMERICAN QUEEN ANNE–STYLE HOUSE

Floor plan shows a free flow of space from one room to another and large openings between rooms.

The hall contains the main staircase, ample room for furniture and decorative items, and a fireplace.

Pocket doors may be installed to enable the large openings between rooms to be closed on occasion.

Porches, verandahs, piazzas, or other covered outdoor spaces play an important part in the design and the use of the house.

Specialized storage rooms including storage for china, or a butler's pantry, first appear in middle-class houses.

Indoor plumbing appears consistently to provide central heating, hot and cold running water, and sanitary drainage.

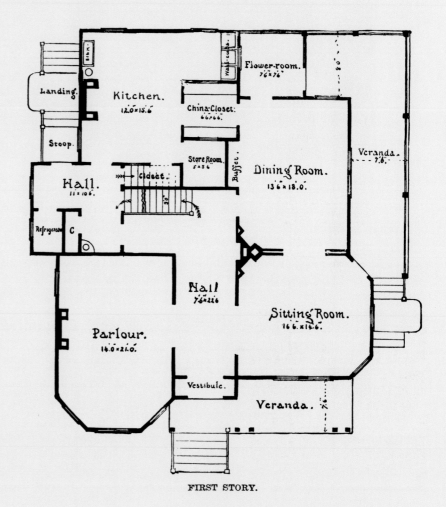

FIRST STORY.

FRONT ELEVATION.

Images from Dwellings for Village and Country, *by S. B. Reed, originally published by O. Judd & Co., New York in 1885; reprinted by Dover Publications, 1999.*

Hipped roof with projecting gables on one or more sides.

Decoration within the gable ends, which might include half-timbering or patterned shingles.

Decorative brickwork patterns on tall chimneys.

Upper floor shingles will flare or "kick" out over the line of the first floor exterior wall.

Different textures are important on the building, even if everything is made of the same material.

Shingles in several patterns, clapboards, and flush-boarding are all used with wood to give the surface interest and highlight architectural features.

Windows have upper sash of small decorative panes or stained glass.

Grouped windows, especially in gables, form a continuous row or band.

Windows are different sizes, patterns, and shapes from one another.

Double front doors have large windows in them.

Porches and balconies have turned columns and railings.

INDEX